AA

ORDNANCE SURVEY
LEISURE GUIDE

PEAK DISTRICT

Produced jointly by the Publishing Division of the
Automobile Association and the Ordnance Survey

Cover: Monsal Dale Viaduct

Title page: stone-walling in Derbyshire
Contents page: a Glasgow Corporation tram
Introductory page: High Tor and the Derwent Valley

Editors: Russell P O Beach, Rebecca Snelling

Art Editor: Dave Austin

Design Assistants: John Breeze, KAG Design

Consultant for the Peak National Park:
Roland Smith, Head of Information Services

Editorial contributors: Roy Christian, MBE (A to Z
Gazetteer); Clarence Daniel (Peakland Customs); Dr
Trevor Elkington (Wildlife of the Peak); Roger Flindall
(Lead Mining in the Peak); Mark Richards (Walks);
Ken Smith (Man and the Landscape); Roland Smith
(The Story of a National Park, A Day in the Life of a
Ranger and the Gazetteer short features)

Picture researcher: Wyn Voysey

Original photography: Malc Birkett

Typeset by Avonset, Midsomer Norton, Bath.
Printed in Great Britain by Butler & Tanner, Frome,
Somerset.

Maps extracted from the Ordnance Survey's 1:63,360
Tourist Series, 1:25,000 Pathfinder Series and
1:250,000 Routemaster Series, with the permission of
Her Majesty's Stationery Office. Crown Copyright
reserved.

Additions to the maps by the Cartographic Dept of the
Automobile Association and the Ordnance Survey.

Produced by the Publishing Division of the Automobile
Association.

Distributed in the United Kingdom by the Ordnance
Survey, Southampton, and the Publishing Division of
the Automobile Association, Fanum House,
Basingstoke, Hampshire RG21 2EA.

The contents of this publication are believed correct at
the time of printing. Nevertheless, the Publishers cannot
accept responsibility for errors or omissions, or for
changes in details given.

Reprinted with amendments 1990
First edition 1987

AA ISBN 0 86145 492 8 (hardback)
AA ISBN 0 86145 491 X (softback)
OS ISBN 0 31900 109 1 (hardback)
OS ISBN 0 31900 108 3 (softback)

Published by the Automobile Association and the
Ordnance Survey.

PEAK DISTRICT

Contents

Using this Book

The entries in the Gazetteer have been carefully selected to reflect the interest and variety of the Peak District although for reasons of space it has not been possible to include every community. A number of small villages are described under the entry for a larger neighbour, and these can be found by using the index.

Each entry in the A to Z Gazetteer has the atlas page number on which the place can be found and its National Grid reference included under the heading. An explanation of how to use the National Grid is given on page 78.

Beneath many of the entries in the Gazetteer are listed AA-recommended hotels, guesthouses, camp sites, garages and self-catering accommodation in the immediate vicinity. Hotels and camp sites are also given an AA classification.

◇ **Please note:** The use of this symbol in this reprint indicates that the establishment is no longer in the AA scheme (it may even have closed) and the AA is therefore unable to verify the particulars.

HOTELS

1-star	Good hotels and inns, generally of small scale and with good furnishings and facilities.
2-star	Hotels with a higher standard of accommodation. There should be 20% with private bathrooms or showers.
3-star	Well-appointed hotels. Two-thirds of the bedrooms should have private bathrooms or showers.
4-star	Exceptionally well-appointed hotels offering high standards of comfort and service. All bedrooms should have private bathrooms or showers.
5-star	Luxury hotels offering the highest international standards.

Hotels often satisfy *some* of the requirements for higher classifications than that awarded.

Red-star	Red stars denote hotels which are considered to be of outstanding merit within their classification.
Country House Hotel	A hotel where a relaxed informal atmosphere prevails. Some of the facilities may differ from those at urban hotels of the same classification.

SELF CATERING

These establishments, which are all inspected on a regular basis, have to meet minimum standards in accommodation, furniture, fixtures and fittings, services and linen.

GUESTHOUSES

These are different from, but not necessarily inferior to, AA-appointed hotels, and they offer an alternative for those who prefer inexpensive and not too elaborate accommodation. They all provide clean, comfortable accommodation in homely surroundings. Each establishment must usually offer at least six bedrooms and there should be a general bathroom and a general toilet for every six bedrooms without private facilities. Parking facilities should be reasonably close.

Other requirements include:
Well maintained exterior; clean and hygienic kitchens; good standard of furnishing; friendly and courteous service; access at reasonable times; the use of a telephone and full English breakfast.

CAMP SITES

1-pennant	Site licence; 10% of pitches for touring units; site density not more than 30 per acre; 2 separate toilets for each sex per 30 pitches; good quality tapwater; efficient waste disposal; regular cleaning of ablutions block; fire precautions; well-drained ground.
2-pennant	All one-pennant facilities plus: 2 washbasins with hot and cold water for each sex per 30 pitches in separate washrooms; warden available at certain times of the day.
3-pennant	All two-pennant facilities plus: one shower or bath for each sex per 30 pitches, with hot and cold water; electric shaver points and mirrors; all-night lighting of toilet blocks; deep sinks for washing clothes; facilities for buying milk, bread and gas; warden in attendance by day, on call by night.
4-pennant	All three-pennant facilities plus: a higher degree of organisation than one–three pennant sites; attention to landscaping; reception office; late-arrivals enclosure; first aid hut; shop; routes to essential facilities lit after dark; play area; bad weather shelter; hard standing for touring vans.
5-pennant	A comprehensive range of services and equipment; careful landscaping; automatic laundry; public telephone; indoor play facilities for children; extra facilities for recreation; warden in attendance 24 hours per day.

WALKS

The walks in this book have been carefully planned to suit families but a few need particular care if young children are in the party. Potential hazards are highlighted in the text.

It is always advisable to go well-equipped with suitable clothing and refreshment, and, as an extra precaution, a compass.

Please observe The Country Code at all times.

PEAK DISTRICT
Introduction

*For centuries seekers after fortune have been lured to
the Peak District by promises of mineral wealth –
lead ore, Blue John and the decorative Ashford
marble. Ironically, those diligent searchers missed the
greatest treasure of all – the richly-varied landscape
beneath which they worked. Within a huge
horseshoe of stern gritstone – the Dark Peak – lie
the pastoral summits and slopes of the limestone
White Peak, laced with rivers sparkling through
deep dales. Great houses stand in parkland on the
banks of the Wye, a world of caves and mines lies
deep in the ground and all around are legacies of an
industrial past. Written by people who live in the
Peak, and backed by the AA's research expertise and
the Ordnance Survey's mapping, this guide is as
useful to those who return to the area year after year
as it is to the first-time visitor.*

Man and the Landscape

Modern visitors to the Peak District are attracted to the rugged scenery of the gritstone Dark Peak and the more gentle limestone White Peak. Many, particularly walkers in the Dark Peak, are intent on seeing an original wilderness only partially tamed. In fact the Peak District landscape, even at its most remote, is largely man-made. It abounds with evidence of human impact, from the profusion of dry-stone walls to the development of the peat cover, in which humans certainly had a hand. Much of what can be seen occurred in the last few centuries, the result of the Agricultural and Industrial

Millstones were cut from the grit bones of the Dark Peak landscape to be turned by White Peak rivers

Revolutions. But the story of human activity in the Peak District began much earlier.

The first visitors to the Peak arrived a quarter of a million years ago. They followed reindeer into what was then tundra south of the glaciers that covered most of north Britain. The only evidence is a flint hand-axe they left behind at Hopton, near Wirksworth. There are a few hints of occasional hunting visits by Neanderthal Man during the Ice Age between 80,000 and 30,000BC, but it is only from around 12,000 and 10,000BC, at the very end of the glacial period, that visits by humans begin to increase. Temporary camps were made in the many caves and rock-shelters in the limestone valleys of the White Peak. Examples include Dowel and Fox Hole; Thor's Cave and Ossum's Cave in the Dove and Manifold valleys; One Ash Rock-Shelter, in Lathkill Dale; and the evocatively-named Old Woman's House Cave, near Taddington. From these sites have come flint artifacts and bones of reindeer, items lost or abandoned by the departing hunters to remain as mute testimony to the skills of these Upper Palaeolithic (Old Stone Age) people.

As the glaciers retreated (around 10,000BC), red deer and roe deer replaced the reindeer of the Ice Age. Hunting bands of humans followed the deer on to their upland summer pastures, particularly in the Dark Peak. Evidence suggests that Middle Stone Age hunters bettered their chances of hunting success by felling trees and burning vegetation, to improve grass growth and encourage their prey to graze in predictable locations. These activities probably assisted the later spread of the blanket bog on the gritstone uplands, because water collected on the ground instead of being taken up by the trees. In this way, even as early as 7,000BC, humans had begun to leave their mark on the landscape.

First farmers
Farming was introduced before 3000BC and spread fairly rapidly. Herding domesticated sheep and cattle, and growing primitive forms of wheat and barley, replaced hunting and gathering as a way of living. Where the outskirts of Buxton stand today were wooden rectangular houses built by these early farmers, and elsewhere earthen long mounds were constructed for their dead. For the first time there was permanent settlement on the limestone plateau where the less dense tree cover and the light soils suited the primitive range of farm tools available.

By 2000BC mass burials were being made in chambers built of enormous stones incorporated into large circular cairns like that at Minninglow, an enormous burial mound which imposes itself, even as a ruin, upon the landscape of the southern Peak. Ceremonial monuments were also built for the first time. The two henges of Abror Low, the 'Stonehenge of the North', with its circle of fallen stones, and the Bull Ring at Dove Holes, appear to oversee separate territories divided by the River Wye. Whether built as markets or fairs, as meeting places or locations for ceremony and ritual, their precise function remains enigmatic.

Bronze Age people settled widely in the White Peak, and dozens of burial mounds dot the limestone hilltops. Over 400 Peak District barrows were excavated by Thomas Bateman, in the middle years of the 19th century (the collection of grave goods accumulated by this energetic Victorian antiquarian is now housed in Sheffield City

Circles in time. The ancient henge monument of Arbor Low is echoed in form by a more recent dew pond

Museum). Apart from barrows, few other remains can be found on the limestone, and the most complete and best preserved remains of Bronze Age settlement are found on Stanton Moor and on the dramatic gritstone edges east of the Derwent, where plentiful remnants have been preserved since about 1000BC by the very inhospitality of these bleak moorlands.

Until recently hill-forts were thought to be a feature of the Iron Age, prior to the Roman occupation. However, work at Mam Tor, near Castleton, now suggests that it was occupied in the early Bronze Age, much earlier than was previously thought possible. Peak District hill-forts may have been a response to social pressures in the later Bronze Age when the gritstone moorlands were being abandoned, rather than a later Iron Age phenomenon. At Harborough Rocks there are hints of Iron Age activity in about 500BC, and an earthwork enclosure on Tideswell Moor is clipped by the later Bathamgate Roman road, allowing it to be dated to the pre-Roman period. But the overall evidence is sparse, perhaps indicating that this was a virtually depopulated border country.

The Romans
This apparent isolation was rudely shattered by the Roman invasion of Britain. In the early 70sAD the Romans moved north from the River Trent and occupied the Peak, primarily to exploit the rich deposits of lead for which the area was known. With customary Roman efficiency, two forts were established, one at Brough (*Navio*) and another on the western fringes of the Peak at *Melandra* (*Ardotalia*), Glossop. A system of roads was constructed surrounding and crossing the Peak, linking the forts with those established at other points around the region.

The centre of Roman lead production is thought to have been *Lutudarum*, which has not been found but was probably in the Wirksworth and

Carsington area. The name has been found on Roman pigs (or ingots) of lead. In the wake of the military came civilian settlement. Small farmsteads were established at The Burrs, Chelmorton, at Chee Tor above Millers Dale with its impressive terraced fields, and at Roystone Grange, Ballidon, where extensive remains of a native Roman farmstead and its associated field systems can be seen. Buxton was established, as the spa-town of *Aquae Armenetia*, but the only other substantial civilian settlements were those that built up around the Roman forts, to meet the various needs of the troops stationed there.

With the removal of the Roman legions at the beginning of the 5th century, the Peak District sank into the relative obscurity of the Dark Ages. Little is known of the people of the Peak until the late 7th century, when the 'Tribal Hidage', drawn up to assess the taxable value of the kingdom of Mercia and its dependents, has a reference to the Pecsaetan, 'the dwellers of the Peak'. It is their remains that have been found in pagan burial places, in barrows such as Wigber Low and Benty Grange, complete with weapons of iron and ornaments of precious metals. Major events occurred in and around the area in the 9th and 10th centuries AD, but there is little physical evidence to record the Anglo-Saxon conquest of Anglian Mercia in 827, the Viking raids (which culminated in their annexation of Mercia in 874 and the founding of Derby), or the reconquest of the region by Edward the Elder in 920. In that year Edward built a fortress at Bakewell, where he received the submission of various northern leaders. Isolated monuments like the Grey Ditch at Bradwell, a bank and ditch closing off a valley route south into Mercia, may date from this period, reflecting the one-time border between Mercia and its northern neighbour Northumbria.

Stone crosses
One outstanding survival from the period is the numerous fragments of decorated stonework, particularly crosses. Thought to be mainly early Christian preaching crosses, used before churches were built, examples can be found in the churchyards of Hope, Eyam, Bakewell and Bradbourne. Highly-decorated tombstone slabs can also be found at Wirksworth and at Bakewell.

Norman castles
Twenty years after the Norman Conquest, William ordered a survey of his kingdom, the results of which were recorded in *Domesday*. Many Peakland villages were included, suggesting that occupation of the Peak was quite extensive by the 11th century AD. One of the lasting monuments to the Conquest is the gaunt ruin of Peveril Castle overlooking Castleton. It was given initially to William Peveril, the Conqueror's illegitimate son, and Castleton was developed as a planned town at its foot, though it never prospered. The castle also served as a hunting lodge for forays out into the Royal Forest of the Peak, which covered some 40 square miles of surrounding country. An example of the more usual motte and bailey castle can be seen at Pilsbury, near Hartington.

The Middle Ages
The 12th and 13th centuries were generally a time of expansion in medieval England. But a series of bad harvests and the Black Death in the mid-14th century wiped out up to a third of the population,

Against this superb Saxon cross the fine old church at Eyam is a brash newcomer

Perhaps the most enduring of man's works in the Peak are the narrow fields with which he striped the hills

and many villages were either deserted or deliberately depopulated, as landlords converted their lands to sheep and wool production.

Sheep featured large in the economy of the Peak in the 12th to the 14th centuries, when monastic houses outside the area established sheep granges on the verdant grassland of the White Peak. Virtually every modern farm with 'grange' in its name originated in this way, having originally been worked by lay bretheren and local labour.

Those villages which were left after the 14th-century recession prospered. In Tideswell the magnificent Perpendicular parish church, known as the 'Cathedral of the Peak', was built almost completely in the 14th century from the profits of wool and lead. In many areas the undulating 'ridge and furrow' of medieval fields can still be seen. Some of the finest examples occur around Bradbourne, Fenny Bentley and Tissington, and in the Lower Manifold Valley around Throwley, where particularly extensive terraces of lynchets have survived, a means of creating level ground from the hillslopes.

Enclosures
In many ways the present-day character of the Peak District landscapes began to develop in the 17th and 18th centuries. This was the period when many of the limestone and gritstone farmhouses, each with their attendant cluster of farm buildings, were built. Medieval open fields were enclosed by agreement and stone walls were built, preserving the characteristic reversed S-shape of medieval ridge and furrow fields. These, seen around villages such as Chelmorton, Litton, Tideswell and Flagg, are an essential part of the Peakland landscape. They gave rise to Celia Fiennes' comment (in her *Journeys*) that '. . . you see neither hedge nor tree but only low drye stone walls round some ground. . . .' At the time she was writing, in about 1700, much of

Hikers resting their packs at a stone packhorse bridge, by which an ancient equestrian trading route crosses the tumbling River Goyt

Bridge building in the Peak reached its height when Monsal Dale was spanned by this majestic viaduct

the Peak District was unenclosed. A century later, with the Enclosure Movement in full swing, enormous areas were being divided into the geometric field patterns that can be seen today. Hundreds of miles of stone walls were constructed as heath and common grazing land were enclosed and spread with tons of locally-produced lime to encourage the growth of sweet Peakland grass for cattle and sheep.

Road and rail

The Peak was slow to lose its remoteness. Many pack-horse routes, still visible on the moors east of the Derwent, crossed the Peak in the medieval period and were used by long trains of animals carrying salt and cheese from Cheshire and the west, returning with lime, lead and stone. Pack-horse bridges, narrow with low parapets to avoid the panniers, survive at Edale and elsewhere. Good roads though were sadly lacking. Indeed, Celia Fiennes, in her journey through Derbyshire, asserted '. . . you are forced to have Guides as in all parts of Derbyshire . . .' and '. . . the common people know not above 2 or 3 miles from their home. . . .' In the

second half of the 18th century, turnpike roads began to make their way through the area, providing for the first time a reasonable road-transport system along which agricultural and mineral produce could be moved more rapidly and cheaply. With no canals through the region, the roads carried considerable traffic until, in the 19th century, an alternative was offered by the railways. The Cromford and High Peak Railway was a direct competitor after its opening in 1831, particularly for bulky minerals.

Lead-mining

The Industrial Revolution made its mark even in the remote fastnesses of the Peak in the 18th and 19th centuries. Lead production, important for centuries but worked only on a relatively small scale, increased rapidly with advances in smelting technology. This led to a proliferation of mines and engine houses, furnaces and condensers, and large tracts of ravaged countryside bear testimony to the industrial exploitation. Limestone quarrying, initially on a small scale to provide for local needs, also expanded, both as a result of the increased local agricultural demand for lime and with the increased ability of the companies to move the finished product out of the Peak District. Gritstone quarrying flourished, for building materials and for grindstones and millstones, large numbers of which can still be found abandoned in quarries that no longer ring to the sound of the mason's hammer.

The Peak District landscapes have always proved attractive to man. The rugged gritstone moors have provided hunting and pasture, while the more mellow limestone has offered plentiful grazing and the opportunity to grow crops in sheltered locations. Both have provided enormous quantities of minerals over the centuries, to supply and sustain developing agriculture and industry. The signs of this human impact on the landscapes are everywhere, waiting to be appreciated.

The Story of a National Park

During the 1930s life in the great industrial cities which flank the southern Pennines was grim. The country was in the depths of the Depression, unemployment was soaring, and the post Great War promise of 'a land fit for heroes' had a hollow, empty ring. The teeming populations of Manchester, Sheffield, Stoke-on-Trent and Derby found little to cheer them in the pervading gloom. But there was one escape route from their back-to-back terraces. Beyond the smoky streets the blue, misty outline of the moors beckoned. The Peak District had long been an important 'lung' for the recreation of city dwellers, who flooded out at weekends and holidays by bus and train in huge numbers.

Recording this phenomenon in *The Untutored Townsman's Invasion of the Country*, Professor Cyril Joad wrote: 'In our day, hiking has replaced beer as the shortest cut out of Manchester, as turning their backs upon the cities which their fathers made, armies of young people make sorties at any and every opportunity into the countryside.' Patrick Monkhouse, in *On Foot in the Peak* published in 1932, confirmed: 'The movement which has brought young townsfolk out on to the moors has hardly a parallel elsewhere in Britain. For an hour on Sunday mornings it looks like Bank Holiday in the Manchester stations, except that families do not go to Blackpool for Whit-week in shorts. Southcountrymen gasp to look at it.'

Forbidden ground

However, as Professor Joad recounted, on all this country there was laid 'the curse of the keeper'. Vast areas of the highest, most spectacular moors of the Peak District were strictly preserved for the rearing, management and shooting of red grouse, or as water-gathering grounds by the municipal authorities. Stern-faced gamekeepers were

employed to keep the ramblers off the moors of Kinder Scout, Bleaklow and the eastern moors. The moorland edges were dotted with 'Trespassers will be Prosecuted' signs, which the ramblers called 'wooden liars' because they had no power in law. Straying off one of the few footpaths could result in an encounter with a keeper not averse to bully-boy eviction tactics.

Walking guides of the day actually warned ramblers where to watch out for unfriendly gamekeepers. Monkhouse, describing a short cut from South Head to Edale Cross on Kinder in *On Foot in the Peak* said a gamekeeper could be seen 'on populous Sundays' sitting with a dog and a gun on the side of South Head. 'His presence is usually an adequate deterrent, and the gun has not yet been used.' The classic walkers guide, *Across the Derbyshire Moors* by John Derry, warned in 1926, 'Nothing keeps alive the spirit of revolt and iconoclasm so fiercely as a refusal to the general community of the use of their eyes over beautiful remote tracts of the earth, under the plea of private ownership.' The owners were determined to keep the ramblers off, and some even went to the length of publishing photographs of walkers on Kinder

Scout in local newspapers, with a reward for their identification. More liberal landowners issued permits for walkers.

Gaining access

Pressure for access to these high and lonely places grew through the 1920s and 1930s in the wake of unemployment and the new political awareness of the working class. Protest rallies, some attended by up to 10,000 ramblers, were held in the Winnats Pass and Cave Dale, near Castleton. They called for free access to mountain and moorland, and significantly, for the creation of National Parks. Eventually and inevitably, the issue came to a head with the celebrated Mass Trespass on to Kinder Scout on 24 April 1932. About 400 ramblers set out from Hayfield with the well-publicised intention of trespassing on the forbidden moorland of Kinder. As they left the confines of William Clough and approached the plateau edge below Sandy Heys, they encountered groups of keepers, and scuffles broke out. As a result, six ramblers were arrested, charged with riotous assembly and assault, and five received prison sentences of between two and six months at Derby Assizes.

Kinder Scout, where only privileged feet trod before 400 walkers defied owners in a battle for free access to the moors. Their protests helped make possible today's National Park, whose millstone symbol recalls both local grit and an old Peakland industry

Many people have since questioned the need for, and effectiveness of, the Mass Trespass, which was followed by others that received much less publicity. But there can be no doubt that it proved to be one of the most important catalysts for the National Parks and access to the countryside legislation which followed World War II. In his report on National Parks to the post-war Labour government, Sir Arthur Hobhouse pointed out: 'The controversy over access to uncultivated lands reaches its height in the Peak, where landowners may draw their most remunerative rents from the lease of grouse moors, and where at the same time large areas are sterilised for water catchment. Many of the finest moorlands, where thousands wish to wander, are closed against 'trespassers' and an altercation with a gamekeeper may often mar a day's serenity. A National Park in the Peak District will not justify its name unless this problem is satisfactorily solved.'

Upper Derwent, where reservoirs and afforestation have softened a stern landscape and added extra dimensions to a naturally varied countryside

Access was not the only reason why the Peak became the first British National Park.

Within two years of its inception in 1951, the first agreement allowing free access, except for a few days during the grouse-shooting season, had been signed. Today, 76 square miles of the northern and eastern moors, including the infamous 'battlegrounds' of the 1930s, are subject to agreements between the National Park and landowners. Access land in the Peak still accounts for 60 per cent of the total in the country.

Hobhouse had reported: '. . . beyond its intrinsic qualities, the Peak has a unique value as a National Park, surrounded as it is on all sides by industrial towns and cities. Sheffield, Manchester, Huddersfield, Derby and The Potteries lie on its borders; indeed, it is estimated that half the population of England lives within 60 miles of Buxton. There is no other area which has evoked more strenuous public effort to safeguard its beauty

. . . Its very proximity to the industrial towns renders it as vulnerable as it is valuable.' Those threats included mineral extraction, regarded by Hobhouse as the most serious menace and still the greatest threat to the National Park today; the flooding of valleys for reservoirs; afforestation by alien conifers; and the insidious spread of suburbs.

What is a National Park?

There are still many misconceptions about our National Parks. Unlike those of the USA and most other countries, British National Parks are not owned by the nation. The majority of land in them is in private hands, their being the home and workplace of local people. The usually-accepted definition is that first coined by architect and planner John Dower, in his seminal 1945 report which laid down the blueprint for our Parks. A National Park is:

'An extensive area of beautiful and relatively wild country in which, for the nation's benefit and by appropriate national decision and action,
   (a) the characteristic landscape beauty is strictly preserved,
   (b) access and facilities for public open-air enjoyment are amply provided,
   (c) wildlife and buildings and places of architectural and historic interest are suitably protected while
   (d) established farming use is effectively maintained.'

The National Park is administered by a local-government authority known as the Peak Park Joint Planning Board. This body takes on the planning powers of the six county councils in whose area it lies, and also provides facilities and services for the estimated 20 million visitors it receives every year. Two-thirds of the governing Board represent local county and district councils, while the remaining is appointed by the Government to look after national interests (although most members are also local people). Approximately 75 per cent of its income comes from central-government grant support, and the rest from local rates.

Schemes and services

One of the other benefits which came from access agreements was the creation of the Park's highly-respected Ranger Service (see page 27), which acts as the essential link between locals and visitors.

Another vital link between the visiting public (most of whom still come from the surrounding cities), and the National Park is the Information Service, which runs eight centres throughout the Park and produces a wide range of publications, walks and talks. Here the second duty of providing facilities for public enjoyment is met, and the Park's residential-study centre at Losehill Hall in Castleton caters for those who wish to learn more about this landscape.

Nevertheless the National Park's first duty is as a planning authority, and it has exercised its planning role in several innovative ways designed to benefit both visitor and local alike. An example of this was the Goyt Valley Traffic Scheme, which closed off a popular valley to traffic at busy times and provided alternatives, a system since copied in the Upper Derwent Valley.

Right: many of the small, informal walled fields in the Peak date from before the 18th-century Enclosures, and a few are of Celtic origin

Bridges, embankments and cuttings add interest to long and evenly-graded trails that have been established for cyclists and walkers along old railway trackbeds throughout the National Park

Railway trails

When two railway lines crossing the White Peak plateau closed within a few weeks of each other in the late 1960s, the Peak Board stepped in to create the popular Tissington and High Peak Trails, thus preserving them and providing walkers, riders and cyclists with routes across some of the Park's finest scenery. Bicycles can be hired on the Tissington Trail (the former Ashbourne to Buxton route), and on the High Peak Trail (once the Cromford and High Peak line). The authority has since also bought the former Midland line to create the Monsal Trail along the Wye Valley. John Ruskin protested at the building of the Monsal Viaduct across the Wye; today it is one of the railway structures which have been considered well worth preserving in the conversion of the old routes.

Stone tents

A number of farm barns have also been converted – into 'stone tents' or 'camping barns', offering simple overnight accommodation for a small fee. They offer a space to sleep, a place to wash, a cooking area (but no cooking equipment), and shelter. As well as providing a roof for walkers and cyclists, they also make use of buildings which have become redundant for farm use but still contribute a good deal to the landscape.

Integration

The 'Routes for People' scheme in the White Peak area sought to separate the potentially dangerous mixture of heavy quarry traffic from holiday motorists in an integrated network of specialist routes, with picnic areas and waymarked walks.

The theme of integration has been expanded further in recent years to cover whole village communities in the 'Integrated Rural Development' programme (IRD) in Longnor and Monyash. A pooling of resources and a willingness to co-operate and compromise has led to an exciting departure in

The train has gone but the viaduct remains as a superb viewpoint from which Monsal Trail walkers can appreciate the beautiful Wye Valley

countryside planning and management. Farmers have been paid, not for harmful chemical sprays, but for the number of wild flowers in their hay meadows; not for alien post-and-wire fences, but for the maintenance of their traditional and attractive dry-stone walls.

Patrick Monkhouse wrote half a century ago that people had never been more conscious of the beauty of hills and dales, and never thought it more important that beauty should remain beautiful. Surely those sentiments still hold true.

Wildlife of the Peak

The Peak District – at the southern end of the Pennine Chain – contrasts markedly in scenery and wildlife with the lowlands which surround it. Within the National Park too are striking variations in scenery, caused by differences in the underlying rocks.

At the centre is the 'White Peak', a region of Carboniferous limestone measuring roughly 10 miles from the River Hamps in the west to the River Derwent in the east. Much of the region forms a plateau of some 1,000ft altitude, scored by a network of steep-sided dales cut by water erosion, but now often dry. Unlike the plateau itself, they are rich reservoirs of wildlife.

Underground, as in all limestone regions, the dissolving action of rainwater has formed many channels and caverns. Some have become popular tourist attractions, while others can only be seen by the intrepid caver.

Surrounding the White Peak is a horseshoe of moorland known as the 'Dark Peak', a dramatic landscape formed by massive sandstone rocks known as millstone grit – from their usage in the past. This culminates in the dual plateaux of Kinder Scout and Bleaklow, both over 2,000ft.

A perfect example of Peakland habitats, with the craggy crest and grassy slopes of Chrome Hill overlooking riverside woodland and valley pasture alongside the River Dove

In the east of the Park is a series of gritstone escarpments or 'edges' – beloved by climbers – which face across the distant River Derwent towards the limestone. To the west the gritstone forms Axe Edge and The Roaches. Other rocks are seen strikingly exposed in a huge landslip at Mam Tor, near Castleton.

Moorlands of the Dark Peak

Perhaps the most conspicuous feature of the Dark Peak is its heather, which is managed by spring burning to encourage tender new shoots and

Where the going is tough, only the tough survive – like the moorland heathers (top) and cotton grass (upper right). But in their shelter can be found more tender types, like the bog asphodel (right)

enables the ground to support sheep and grouse. In wetter areas the vegetation is dominated by hare's-tail cottongrass, which when fruiting makes the ground look as if it is covered with cotton wool. Drier moorland supports black-fruited bilberry, red-fruited cowberry and the crowberry.

More localised is the cloudberry, a northern species whose raspberry-like leaves and white flowers are seen around Kinder Scout and Bleaklow. Its orange fruit is now rarely found – perhaps because of increased sheep grazing – but last century was harvested for local markets.

The peat on the upper moors is badly eroded – as is obvious to anyone driving over the A57 Snake Pass between Sheffield and Glossop, and even more so to Pennine Way walkers struggling through the loose, sticky masses that cover the surface. Some of the damage may have been caused by widespread fires in recent drought years, or overgrazing by sheep.

On steep slopes below the peat level is rough

grassland which commonly includes tussocky mat-grass tough enough to resist even sheep – but all too often such areas have become poisonous seas of bracken.

Springs and seepage zones are marked by patches of soft rush and often carpeted with *Sphagnum* bog moss, occasionally sharing the damp habitat with bog asphodel and the insectivorous sundew.

Hidden inhabitants

At first glance the casual visitor may find the moors bleak, but they have a rich variety of insects and other small animals. Most conspicuous are some of the larger moths and their larvae, including the large, hairy, black-and-brown caterpillars of the northern oak eggar, which are often found amongst the heather. The adult has an impressive wingspan of up to 4in. In either form it is easily distinguished from the Emperor moth, which has obvious 'eye' markings on its wings and produces green and black caterpillars.

Butterflies are relatively few. The most characteristic is the green hairstreak, which is often found on flowering bilberry in the late spring.

Moorland birds and their distinctive calls lend a special character to the uplands. The most common breeding species is the meadow pipit, but also found are skylarks and – less commonly – curlews, golden plovers and merlin. Bright colouring and the metallic clatter of its call makes the red grouse one

The Emperor moth's larvae feed on heather

The pastoral White Peak

Views of the White Peak from the A623 road north of Tideswell encompass a panorama of rolling green fields cut by white limestone walls – typical of the plateau and in direct contrast to the country of the Dark Peak. Yet fewer than 200 years ago most of this was covered with heather, and it was only when the open land was enclosed that it began to take on its present, softer complexion. Remnants of White Peak heath survive on the highest ground above Bradwell and Great Longstone, and can also be seen beside the

The lime-loving meadow cranesbill is one of several native geraniums found beside White Peak lanes

of the most obvious species, fairly easily seen as it feeds on the young heather shoots that are its staple diet. Not so obvious are its chicks, whose camouflage blends perfectly with the old heather in which the birds nest.

Of the few mammals that live on the upland, perhaps the most distinctive is the mountain hare. This was re-introduced to Derbyshire during the 19th century and has become well established on Kinder Scout and the eastern moors. In winter it turns completely white.

Peak woodlands

Peak District woodlands survive in a few of the valleys, or 'cloughs', and on the gritstone are dominated by sessile oak with scattered birch – plus rowan and alder alongside streams. Good examples include Padley Wood, which is near Sheffield on the National Trust's Longshaw Estate, as well as Ladybower and Priddock Woods – which overlook Ladybower Reservoir and are both managed by the Derbyshire Wildlife Trust as nature reserves.

Between the trees the ground cover is mainly bilberry and wavy-hair grass, interspersed with several types of fern, and only near streams can there be found more varied flora. Large ant heaps are inhabited by the hairy-eyed wood ant, whose soldiers defend the colony from intruders by spraying formic acid. The oaks themselves are home to many creatures, and in spring support massive hatches of moth caterpillars, a major source of food for blue tits, coal tits and great tits, warblers, redstarts and – encouraged to breed at the limit of their range by nestboxes – pied flycatchers. Other larvae are extracted from the timber by woodpeckers, and the green woodpecker is attracted by wood ants.

Sadly, these interesting remnants of native woodlands and the fine opportunities for natural-history study they present are far outstripped by conifer plantations, which support few ground plants but are of interest as strongholds for the red squirrel and nesting sites for sparrowhawks.

A515 road south of Newhaven.

A few colourful hay meadows survive from the past, and many wild plants are found along the wide roadside verges. In summer the older fields may be yellow with buttercups, while cow parsley and hogweed fringe the lanes with white flowers before making way for the blue of meadow cranesbill – known locally as 'thunderclouds' because it blooms in the July period of thunderstorms.

Strikingly different flora is found in grassland which has colonised along the lines of lead veins or 'rakes', and around their attendant workings. Mineral bands traversing the plateau rise to the surface of the limestone and often run for miles. Many have not been worked for centuries – or at worst, have been disturbed only intermittently – and not even farm animals present a threat, since they are usually prevented from grazing the lead-impregnated vegetation.

One of the most conspicuous plants associated with the rakes is the yellow mountain pansy, while in areas of loose debris during June or July can be found the white flowers of spring sandwort – also known as leadwort because of its habitat.

There are few birds on the White Peak plateau, because the ground-nesting species commonly associated with fields – lapwings, meadow pipits and skylarks, for instance – are unable to withstand the frequent disruption of grass cutting for silage.

Various animals have survived by taking refuge in the dry-stone walls of the field boundaries, including several species of vole and shrew, the stoats and weasels that prey on them, and nesting wheatears and stonechats.

The Dales

The Dales account for only a small proportion of the Peak National Park, but they are its most valuable wildlife resource.

Five of them are included in the Derbyshire

Dales National Nature Reserve – which is managed by the Nature Conservancy Council, Britain's official nature-conservation body. Other areas are protected by the Derbyshire Wildlife Trust and National Trust.

Before exploitation during and prior to the medieval period the dales were naturally wooded, probably with a variety of trees. Nowadays the commonest species in the natural woodlands are ash and elm, though this balance is changing due to the ravages of Dutch elm disease. Closer to villages there are woods planted specifically to provide a crop of timber. Some of these may be almost entirely of ash or sycamore.

Below the leaf canopy in the natural woods is a

Bloody cranesbill grows alongside the Peak Trails

Wheatears are often seen flitting along drystone walls and across the bare hillside scree

wide diversity of plants, including hazel, bird cherry, guelder rose and occasionally such rarities as mountain currant and the early-flowering mezereon. Spring brings colourful displays of bluebells, yellow archangel, sweet woodruff and – on damper soils – the white, clustered stars of the garlic-like ransoms.

Late spring is a good time for bird watching in dales woodland, when the chaffinch and willow warbler are found with the chiff-chaff, wood warbler, spotted flycatcher and both the great-spotted and green woodpecker.

Scrub, also common in the dales, has greatly increased since the rabbit population was reduced by myxomatosis in the 1950s. Hawthorn in particular has reduced interesting grassland to such an extent that much time and energy has been

given to its removal – especially from nature reserves. Other scrub areas – particularly those of hazel – are quite different in character and of much greater interest. Among their rare flora can be found lily of the valley, bloody cranesbill and globeflower.

Grassland slopes

Grassland in the dales is similarly rich in flowers during late spring, with the royal spikes of early-purple orchids and yellow of cowslips painting bright splashes of colour on the valley slopes. Later they are replaced by smaller summer plants – the gold of bird's-foot trefoil and common rock rose contrasting with purple thyme. The most visible of the many insects on the sunny, south-facing slopes are the butterflies, starting early in the season with the orange tip and green hairstreak, which give way to the common blue in summer. Also in this warm, dry habitat is one of the few reptiles to be found in the dales – the harmless slow worm, a snake-like legless lizard which shelters under stones and logs in hot weather.

These grassland areas depend for their continued existence on regular grazing by sheep or cattle, now much less prevalent than formerly.

On some of the steeper slopes – particularly below crags is seen the uncommon limestone fern, which is beautifully delicate in appearance but sufficiently tough to survive the arid conditions that can prevail. Excellent views of these isolated and often inaccessible 'reserves' can be enjoyed from the Monsal Trail, a walk which follows the course of the one-time Midland Railway.

Waterlife

Only a few of the valleys feature permanent rivers – in particular the Dove, Lathkill and Wye, all of which flow through a series of dales. Their trout fishing has been renowned for centuries. Indeed, during 1676 no less an angler than Charles Cotton wrote of the Lathkill in Izaak Walton's *The Compleat Angler*, '. . . it is, by many degrees the purest and most transparent stream that I ever yet saw, either at home or abroad; and breeds, 'tis said, the reddest and best Trouts in England.'

Little has changed. The Lathkill is still one of the country's purest rivers, still supports a wealth of aquatic life from the smallest larvae to the largest fish – and still provides immense pleasure.

River birds in the Peak District include the bright kingfisher, which is seen darting along the streams in search of small fish; the bobbing dipper, which walks underwater to find its prey; and both pied and grey wagtails, constantly engaged in hunting insects along limestone and gritstone banks. Competing with the wagtails are Daubenton's bats, which flit over the water at dusk.

In the northern part of the National Park are several water reservoirs – the best known being the Derwent Valley complex, of which Ladybower is the largest. None is particularly noted for large concentrations of water fowl, but they do provide breeding grounds for teal and winter quarters for pochard, goldeneye and goosander. Common sandpipers breed on the shores.

Unique in having such contrasting scenery and wildlife so close together, the Peak National Park's attractions depend on a fragile web of life that could easily be broken by abuse or thoughtlessness. Only a tiny fraction of the area can be protected as nature reserves, with the fate of the remainder in the hands of owners, farmers and visitors.

Lead Mining in the Peak

Extensive surface remains survive at Magpie Mine, Sheldon, including a 'Cornish' engine house of 1869. Below: a mine team photographed at the turn of the century. The man on the left has a bunch of tallow dips

Lead mining and agriculture were the principle industries in the White Peak from the time of the Roman occupation until the exhausted mines succumbed to cheap imports of foreign lead during the 1870s. The limestone rock is criss-crossed by countless mineral veins, the most common type being 'scrins' which formed where mineralising fluids filled vertical joints a few inches wide in the limestone. 'Rake' veins are similar but much wider, being mineralised faults, whereas 'pipe' veins were formed by the deposition of minerals in natural caverns. Scattered along the courses of these veins are some 30,000 abandoned lead-mine workings, yet these man-made scars have blended back into the landscape and are no longer obtrusive, their aura of mystery heightened by their curious names: Joseph's Dream, Hit or Miss, Hanging Eye, Boggart Hole, Trusty Friend, Wanton Legs, Nell I'll Tickle Thee.

Conditions underground were often cramped, wet and cold, the work being both dangerous and physically exhausting. The miners were of a rough, unhealthy appearance and they spoke a broad dialect, using many specialised mining terms which were unintelligible to visitors from other areas. Daniel Defoe, writing early in the 18th century, described a Wirksworth miner as 'a most uncouth spectacle . . . clothed all in leather . . . lean as a skeleton, pale as a dead corpse'. Women were not employed underground, but many found work 'dressing' ore.

Frequent accidents

Accidents were all too frequent, the worst resulting from explosions of firedamp (methane from the shale strata) such as at Mawstone Mine, Youlgreave, which left eight dead, including three members of a rescue party.

Right: the centre figure of this trio, Mr Fox, was entombed for three days in Townend Mine Left: small, carved figure of a female ore dresser. Below: bronze dish that was once the standard measure of ore in the Low Peak. It holds some 14 pints

kept there for the measurement of lead ore. It is made of bronze and dates to the reign of Henry VIII, and all the individual dishes belonging to the liberties had to match the contents of this one. Low Peak dishes are rectangular, while those of the High Peak resemble small wooden tubs.

Miners prospecting for veins of lead in the King's Field were authorised 'by the custom of the mine to dig, delve, search, subvert, and overturn all manner of grounds, lands, meadows, closes, pastures, mears and marshes, for ore mines of

Laws and customs

Many miners worked at their own small mines and had a ruggedly independent way of life, being literally a law unto themselves. A code of customs which governed every aspect of lead mining had developed gradually over the centuries and was first written down as early as 1288. In each 'liberty' (roughly equivalent to a township) these zealously defended customs were administered by courts consisting of elected miners, supervised by a steward and barmaster appointed by the Lords of the Mineral Field. The latter represented the interests of the Crown, which claimed many mineral rights and revenues. Tithe was paid to the Church. The tribunal of miners made and administered the unique laws by which the industry was governed, becoming virtually independent of all civil law, conducting inquests in the event of fatalities, and exercising the right to punish miners guilty of crimes against their fellows. The theft of ore was a very serious offence, and the first and second convictions were punished by fines of 3s 4d and 6s 8d respectively, but the law for a third conviction decreed that the guilty person had his right hand impaled to the winding structure at the shaft top.

The laws, customs, privileges and entitlements of the industry were listed in a *Rhymed Chronicle* composed by Edward Manlove, a Steward of the Low Peak Courts at Wirksworth, where the Grand Jury met in the Moot Hall. The Standard Dish is

whose inheritance soever they be; dwelling-houses, orchards and gardens excepted'. Other exceptions included highways and churchyards. Various conditions were usually observed by a miner staking a claim, and after the barmaster and two jurymen had confirmed his 'title', he was able to proceed without seeking consent from the land-owner. He could also proceed without permission from anybody, under 'squatter's rights'. If, however, he failed to ratify his claim by producing lead, he was under obligation to redress any damage caused by his excavations. If successful, he was entitled to cut down timber required for his mining operations, and had access to the nearest highway and running water. The verbal laws were compounded into an Act of Parliament which became law in 1851 and 52.

Early history

North of Ballidon at Roystone Grange archaeological excavations have revealed a Roman wall constructed over an opencast lead vein working. The only other evidence of such early mining is the Roman pigs of lead found scattered about the country; inscriptions on these show that they came from *Lutudarum* (perhaps the Roman name for the Peak District) and did not contain silver. After the Roman occupation had ended, mining presumably continued on a smaller scale from opencast sites on the more prominent veins. In 1086 *Domesday* listed seven 'lead works' in

Derbyshire, although these were probably smelting sites. Odin Mine at Castleton is recorded as early as 1280, and by 1470 there was underground mining at the Nestus Mines, Matlock.

Driving the soughs

By 1600 some of the richest rake veins had already been worked out down to the natural water table. Effective pumping equipment was not available, so the answer was to dig drainage levels – locally called soughs (pronounced suffs). The first was made during 1632-51 by a Dutch drainage expert, Sir Cornelius Vermuyden, to drain Gang Mine at Cromford. Later soughs had to be progressively deeper and longer, lowering the water table throughout vast areas and making possible new eras of prosperity for the richest mining fields at Wirksworth, Winster, Alport and Eyam.

There were few aids to the work – the earliest documented use of gunpowder in British mining was at Bailey Croft Sough, Wirksworth, in 1672, but its danger and expense encouraged miners to persist with traditional techniques. Levels were driven through hard ground using a hammer and pick to cut a succession of sweeping parallel grooves in the 'forefield' (or tunnel face), which was advanced only about two inches per shift.

A sequence of soughs was driven into each productive mineral field – at Gang Mine, the Dutchman's Level was soon made redundant by the slightly deeper Bates Sough, which was in turn superseded by Cromford Sough. Begun in about 1672, Cromford Sough eventually attained a length of three miles by 1800. The outflow from Cromford Sough helped to power Arkwright's cotton mill until most of its water was taken by the even deeper Meerbrook Sough which was started in 1772 and by 1806 had already cost £43,745.

There were once over 100 steam engines in Peak District mines, some used for winding and ore-crushing rather than pumping. But their success was limited since coal was so expensive and few lead mines could afford the running costs. In contrast the enormous cost of a major sough was underwritten by wealthy speculators who hoped to recoup their outlay by receiving a proportion of the ore obtained from the numerous mines thereby relieved.

This drainage sough is easily accessible beside the path in Lathkill Dale, and dates from around 1800

Mill Close, Britain's largest lead mine, had produced 430,000 tons of ore by 1938, when it flooded out

Water pressure engines (powered by water falling down the mine shaft and flowing out along a sough) and waterwheels both used a cheap source of power, but often proved impractical in the Peak District, where surface water supplies tend to fail during the summer. A waterwheel installed at Lathkill Dale Mine in 1836 was 52ft in diameter, and at the adjacent Mandale Mine a 35ft diameter wheel was supplied by an aqueduct, the columns of which still cross that picturesque valley.

Riches or ruin

Lead mining was always a financial gamble because of the unpredictability of the veins, which could suddenly 'pinch' out to nothing or 'belly' into a rich pipe. The latter occurred at Ball Eye Mine, Bonsall, where the miners found a 'mass of lead' 50ft high and 120ft wide, worth £12,000. Veins were frequently cut off by lava flows or faults: at Hucklow the High Rake Mining Company lost over £19,000 sinking a shaft 720ft through volcanic rock without meeting the hoped-for limestone strata. Sometimes natural caverns were met and one found at Ball Eye Mine before 1661 contained a mammoth's skull – which greatly puzzled the miners. The workings of adjacent mines frequently intersected underground, and the ensuing legal disputes nearly drove the shareholders to despair. In 1833, after the Magpie workings had broken into Great Redsoil Mine at Sheldon, both sides lit sulphurous fires underground to smoke out their opponents. Three miners died.

By the 19th century veins were becoming exhausted and the odds were stacked against mining speculations. However, a few large ore strikes still occurred, and the legendary Gang Mine made a profit of £8,067 in 1813. The more usual story was of decline: Gregory Mine at Ashover – which had yielded £15,024 profit during 1772 – closed in 1803 after a series of large losses and the nearby Overton Mine suffered a similar fate.

Speculation reached fever pitch during the 1850s after it became possible to form limited liability companies. Many very dubious enterprises were launched and the gullible shareholders fleeced: there was even a project to mine gold in Lathkill Dale – nothing seemed impossible. Eventually the investors became wary and, as a result of a drastic fall in the price of lead ore, nearly all mines were

Visitors to Peak Cavern, at Castleton, can explore a curious underground canal by boat

abandoned before 1900. Mill Close Mine at Darley Dale survived this general decline, having been re-opened in 1859 by Edward Miller Wass, who installed efficient steam engines and struck a vast quantity of ore. By the time Mill Close was flooded out in 1938, it had produced 430,000 tons.

The last attempt to mine lead in Derbyshire was in 1952. Some 200,000 tons of fluorspar are mined annually near Eyam, yielding 4,000 tons of lead ore. Calcite is extracted from Long Rake near Youlgreave, and limestone at Middleton-by-Wirksworth! Along the western flank of the Peak District there are several abandoned copper mines, those at Ecton in the Manifold Valley having yielded a profit of £335,000 during 1760-1817. In addition, silver, zinc, iron and manganese ores, coal, chert, black marble and Blue John were all once part of the rich harvest.

The legacy

Two thousand years of lead mining have left the Peak District riddled with shafts, now mostly collapsed, or capped for safety, although caution is still required when walking in the former mining areas. The courses of scrins and rakes are often delineated by rows of grass-covered hillocks with shafts or collapsed hollows every few yards and ruins of the miners' stone sheds ('coes'). Owing to the restrictive effect of the local mining customs and the poorness of the veins, a typical mine was remarkably small, its two or three owners working part-time and getting only about 10 tons of ore a year. Larger mines had engine shafts and winding gear operated by horses working gins.

Opencast lead workings on rakes resemble small gorges (Dirtlow Rake at Castleton is a fine example), but some sites have been devastated when reworked for fluorspar. Many interesting mineral specimens can be found on wasteheaps. The principal lead ore, galena (lead sulphide), is easily distinguished by its high density and silvery metallic lustre when freshly broken.

The chimneys and flues of old lead smelting furnaces can be seen at Meerbrook (near Alderwasley), Stone Edge (at Ashover), Bradwell and Alport. Often the most problematical remains at smelting sites are the lead particles which still permeate the vegetation and can poison livestock.

Abandoned mine workings are usually very unsafe and should never be explored by casual sightseers. Those curious about the underground world will find the Peak's show caves well worth a visit. At Castleton visitors to Speedwell Cavern are taken in a boat along a canal-like level which was driven during the 1770s in an attempt to locate a lead vein. The nearby Blue John and Treak Cliff caves yield a rare ornamental variety of fluorspar called Blue John; whereas Peak Cavern is an impressive natural cave – as is Poole's Cavern at Buxton. Bagshawe Cavern at Bradwell is a natural cave which was discovered when working Mulespinner Mine. Magpie Mine, Sheldon has more surface remains than any other mine in the Peak, and it is now a field study centre run by the Peak District Mines Historical Society. Visitors can see a Cornish engine house dating from 1869 and other extensive surface remains; the main shaft here is 728ft deep and its sough 'tail' (outlet) is conspicuous by the River Wye in Shacklow Wood, Ashford. There is a display of old lead mining equipment at the Tramway Museum, Crich.

Goodluck Mine (in the Via Gellia near Middleton-by-Wirksworth) was driven 150 years ago as a haulage level to serve some productive scrins; it gives visitors the most accurate impression of typical conditions experienced by the ancient miners. At Matlock Bath, the Great Rutland and Masson caverns reveal how Nestus Pipe was exploited during the 1670s, and on High Tor the Fern and Roman caves are opencast rake workings of great antiquity. Royal Cave and Temple Mine are both fluorspar workings dating only from the 1950s, but the former also contains remnants of Speedwell Lead Mine which was itself a show cave by the 1820s. Temple Mine has a display of mining equipment and is associated with the adjacent Peak District Lead Mining Museum at Matlock Bath. The principal exhibit here is a large water-pressure engine dating from 1819.

Peakland Customs

'Today the Peaklanders are as fond of dancing as ever, and although no piper produces eerie music at feast times they can still make a pretty show. The hill country has endowed the youths and maidens with suppleness and they trip it with exceeding grace. . . . Old customs are tenaciously preserved . . . in some places the wells are dressed for the festival of the patron saint. . . .'

(Robert Murray Gilchrist)

Flowers often figure prominently in the folklore of rural areas where customs have lingered from one generation to another. This is particularly true of the custom of dressing wells as an appreciation of the gift of water, an observance largely confined to the Peak District. It is thought to have originated from the culture of Mediterranean countries where water was valued for cleansing, healing and refreshment, and may have been introduced during the Roman occupation of Britain. Wells found to have healing virtues were dedicated to nymphs

Wells dressing at its best. This fine example of floral artistry was created in the village of Hope, Derbyshire

Many hours of hard work go into wells dressing, for results that are exquisite but purely ephemeral

Flowers figure large in many folk traditions, as demonstrated by the headgear of this morris dancer

believed to preside over the waters, as in the instance of *Aquis Armenetia* at Buxton. Christian missionaries weaned their converts from this form of pagan worship of the wells by agreeing that they should be dedicated to saints of the early Church, and so the strewing of flowers to celebrate the festivals of *Floralia* or *Fontinalia* lapsed.

The custom was revived during the early 17th century at Tissington when a certain Mary Twigg is claimed to have resurrected it by hanging festoons of flowers over the village wells in thanksgiving for the population's immunity – attributed to an unfailing supply of pure water – to bubonic plague or drought. This simple gesture was followed later by the creation of geometrical patterns of flowers, ferns, lichens, mosses and other foliage pressed into a background of moist clay.

Boards, which form the basis of the frames, are pierced with holes and studded with nails to key the clay, then placed on trestles or bales of straw to facilitate the work of 'petalling'. Designs drawn on paper are placed on the clay, and the outlines traced through with knitting needles and other improvised tools. This work completed, the paper patterns are placed conveniently for reference. The outlines are then piped with seeds, rice and alder cones, and filled in with more durable vegetable materials such as leaves and lichens. Finally, the delicate work of petalling is carried out. The petals are inserted from the bottom of the picture like tiles on a roof, so that the paler parts are covered by the next and succeeding layers. This also allows rain or moisture to drain off.

Other villages adopted the idea, sometimes after an improved water supply had been introduced – as at Buxton, Wirksworth and Youlgreave. Over the years more have been added to the list. Victorian writers, such as Robert Murray Gilchrist and Joseph Hatton, give the impression that some of the results were crude both in design and execution, but this cannot be imputed to the present generation of floral tableaux. Techniques vary in some villages but the annual displays are of a very high standard and have become major tourist attractions.

Annual wakes

Wells dressing became integrated into the annual Wake, or patronal festival of a village, which celebrated the church's birthday. On Wake-eve a midnight vigil was held in the church to welcome its saint's day, and the following day was a holiday with morris dancing, sports and other entertainments. It was a time of family re-union, when daughters in domestic service and sons apprenticed to trade or agriculture returned to the parental home for a well-deserved holiday. Derbyshire's most popular folk song, *Hayfield Fair*, recalls how the dancers 'played for ale and cakes'. Unfermented ale was the common beverage before tea became cheap and popular, while the Wakes' cake was baked especially for the occasion.

Castleton garlanding

The Victorian novelist R M Gilchrist wrote: '. . . in one of the most remote villages (Castleton) every Oak Apple Day a quaint and pretty pageant enlivens the irregular grey streets'. He further comments that 'gaily dressed children dance what survives of the Morris . . . whilst King Charles and his lady wife . . . ride in state through the quaint streets. His majesty, in cavalier costume, has the upper part of his body covered with a gorgeous bouquet, in shape not unlike a beehive.'

There have been changes to the pattern over the years, for the royal couple were formerly attended by mounted courtiers dressed in Stuart costume, and preceded by a court jester sweeping the road with a besom but making sudden forays into the ranks of the spectators who were treated to acts of buffoonery. Since 1955, the role of the consort has been filled by a female.

The garland is on a crinoline-like frame of hoops decorated with oak leaves laced with garden and meadow flowers, and surmounted by a posy of flowers called the 'queen'. The six village inns take turns to make the garland, which – at the close of the ceremony – is hauled up the church tower and left to be dismantled by the weather. The 'queen' is placed on the nearby war memorial.

The reason the church tower figures is that until 1897 this was how the parishioners showed their appreciation of the bellringers – who also received their annual remuneration from a public collection

Old age and a Christian veneer do little to disguise an ancient significance in Castelton's Garland Day

Personal and poignant reminders in Ilam village church of young girls who died before their time

that was made on the same day.

Kit dressing

Another custom featuring garlands, now no longer observed, was that of Kit Dressing. This was carried out on 1 May when milk-maids decorated their wooden pails (kits) with garlands and trinkets and carried them on their heads in procession. Stephen Glover, the Derbyshire historian, stated that this custom was observed at Baslow during the annual Wakes: 'At Baslow, the rural festival of kit-dressing took place on the 4th of August, and in the present year (1829) was attended by the Baslow Band . . . There were a great number of persons from the surrounding country, and even more distant places, assembled to witness this rural fête.

Funeral garlands

Garlands usually remind us of revelry and rejoicing, but the faded examples preserved in St Giles's Church at Matlock, and those at Ashford-in-the-Water, Ilam and Trusley, are funeral garlands or 'virgin crants', referred to by Shakespeare in relation to the death of Ophelia.

They were bell-like frames of wood decorated with rosettes, ribbons and streamers, and enclosing a personal relic of the deceased girls in whose memory they had been made.

On the occasion of the funeral the garland was carried by friends of the dead girl, and after the service of committal suspended from the rafters of the church above the pew which she had usually occupied. Such garlands were in many churches until congregations complained that they were gathering dust and cobwebs, and even reducing the light. Many churches followed the example of Hope, where in 1749 the churchwardens authorised the payment of 1s. 6d, 'for removing ye garlands to make ye church lighter'.

Funeral clubs

Village societies were established in many rural communities to avoid the indignity of pay-burying and pauper funerals. At pay-buryings the 'bidder' invited friends and neighbours to a funeral, but warned them that they were expected to make some financial contribution. Widows would sit in the doorway to welcome mourners who expressed their condolences and placed their coins in her outstretched apron, or in a basin. By the payment of weekly premiums of one penny or half-penny, the burial societies provided a scale of benefits governed by length of membership and age at death. It was thought that the introduction of the NHS would cancel out the need for funeral clubs, but some have survived to provide generous benefits which keep ahead of inflation.

Cow clubs were a form of insurance against injury or disease of cattle. Premiums were paid on each cow accepted into the society, of which two

Love Feasts, based on meetings of the early Church, originate from 18th-century religious revivalism

members were appointed to assess the value of the animals. Veterinary treatment was also available. Tideswell Cow Club still survives and supplies its members with official badges of membership.

Love feasts

The 18th-century religious revival, spearheaded by the Wesley brothers, converted multitudes of workers employed in mines and mills, farms and factories, and from every stratum of society to a pattern of religious life and worship which inspired them to build 'wayside Bethels' in remote hamlets, villages and industrial centres throughout the country. Like their founders, the preachers continued the principle of field-preaching by organising and conducting camp-meetings and covenant services. These incorporated 'love feasts', based on the meetings of the early Church and associated with the Last Supper. Such gatherings included a communion service in which the elements consisted of bread and water.

The Woodlands love-feast is held annually in a barn at Alport Castles Farm, near the Snake Pass, on the morning of the first Sunday in July.

Rush bearing

This was once a common custom in the Peak

Once a good way to get the church floor recovered, rush bearing has always been associated with celebration and today allows artistic scope too

District, but only Macclesfield Forest Church has retained the ceremony, observed on the nearest Sunday to 12 August. In his *Survey of Derbyshire* (1815), Farey wrote: 'An ancient custom still prevails in Chapel-en-le-Frith, Glossop, Hayfield, Mellor, Peak Forest, and other places in the north of the county, I believe, of keeping the floor of the church and pews therein, constantly strewed or littered with dried rushes; the process of renewing which annually is called the Rush-bearing, and is usually accompanied by much ceremony. The Rush-bearing in Peak Forest is held on Midsummer Eve in each year. In Chapel-en-le-Frith . . . in the latter end of August, on public notice from the churchwardens, of the rushes being mown and properly dried, in some marshy parts of the parish, where the young people assemble, and having loaded the rushes on carts, decorate the same with flowers and ribbons, and attend them to church in procession . . .' Hayfield Churchwarden Accounts have the entries:

    1722. For rushes for church 2s 6d
    1766. Upon the account of the Rush Cart 5s 0d
    At Whitwell, hay mown in the Church Meadows was used, while straw sufficed at Scarcliffe because of the scarcity of rushes.

Clypping the church

This parochial festival has also gradually waned in popularity and is now continued only at Wirksworth and Burbage, near Buxton. 'Clypping' means clasping or embracing the parent church of a parish, when members of daughter churches join with the main congregation for a service. Some churches marked the occasion on Mothering Sunday. At Wirksworth, a procession led by the town band assembles at the market-place, and upon reaching the church continues to make a circuit of the building. The vicar, choristers and congregation clasp hands to form a human chain around the building as they sing. It is held on 8 September, or the nearest Sunday to that date.

At Burbage, near Buxton, a procession commences on the last Sunday in July at the Burbage Institute and marches to the music of a band. Parents and children encircle the church.

Beating the bounds

Hathersage has its 'gospel stone' built into the foundations of a wayside wall. It was one of the sites visited at Rogationtide by clergy, choir and congregation to seek God's blessing on the growing crops and vegetables, and ask His protection from famine, pestilence and other possible adversities. The prefix 'gospel' was variously attached to a tree at Ashover; a lead-mine near Calver; a well at Hayfield; tumulii at Flagg; a brow at Chapel-en-le-Frith; and heaps of stone near Eyam. In his poem '*Hesperides*', Herrick has an allusion to this springtime custom:

    '*Dearest, bury me*
    Under that Holy-Oke, or Gospel Tree,
    Where (though thou see'st not) thou may'st think upon
    Me, when thou yearly go'st procession.'

The religious ceremony appears to have been combined with the civil custom of 'beating the bounds', when children accompanied their parents along the hedges, walls, lanes and streams which surrounded a parish. At strategic points the children were gently struck with canes, so that when they achieved parenthood they would remember the boundaries and be able to inform their own offspring. The reason for this custom was the illiteracy of most residents, to whom maps and written instructions had little meaning.

Padley Chapel pilgrimage

Padley Chapel is a surviving fragment of the ruined mansion of the family of Padley, later occupied by the Eyres and Fitzherberts. The two latter families were long renowned for their allegiance to the pre-Reformation faith, and it was during the reign of Queen Elizabeth that two recusant priests – Robert Ludlam and Nicholas Garlick, a native of Dinting and former master of Tideswell Free Grammar School – were found hiding at Padley on 24 July 1588. All that has survived from the ruins is the old gatehouse and the chapel above. However, the chapel was reprieved from its secular abuses by the Roman Catholic diocese of Nottingham when it undertook restoration in 1932.

A Day in the Life of a Ranger

Northern District Ranger Ian Hurst on patrol, well equipped for any surprises that the unpredictable Dark Peak (inset) may have in store

It is just before 10 am on a Saturday at Fieldhead – the Peak National Park Information Centre and camp site at Edale, in the shadow of the Park's reigning peak, Kinder Scout. The campers are clearing up after breakfast and the first visitors off the early 'Ramblers Route' train from Manchester or Sheffield are cheerfully setting out for the hills with boots, anoraks and bulging rucksacks. Their heavy boots clomp loundly as they stride across the bare floor of the Information Centre to leave their route cards, or check on the latest weather forecast at the desk. A display on the wall warns them that Kinder is on the same latitude as Labrador or Siberia, and they are reminded that the modest 2,088ft mountain can still be a killer.

In a converted barn at the rear of the centre, another group of walkers is gathering. There is an insurance salesman, an engineer, and a couple of unemployed youths. Their equipment is a bit more worn than the average rambler's, but otherwise they are the same, itching to get on the hill. There is one difference, however, because they each wear a shining silver and green badge depicting Peveril Castle – the medieval stronghold of William Peverel, at nearby Castleton. They are part-time Patrol Rangers employed by the Peak National Park at weekends to provide the link between landowners, visitors and the Park authority. But there is much more to being a National Park Ranger than that, as a typical day was to show.

Full-time Ranger

Ian Hurst, Northern District Ranger, walks in – clad in the coveted lovat green sweater and twill breeches of a full-timer – to supervise the morning briefing. Malcolm Padley, a part-timer for nearly 30 years, information assistant and full-time litter warden (he is unofficially known as 'The Chief Womble') for the Park – chalks up the details of each ranger's patrol for the day on a blackboard at the end of the room. For Mike Morton, an architect from Stockport, his typical day will consist of an eight-mile round of Broadlee Bank, Jacob's Ladder, Edale Cross, the Woolpacks, Upper and Nether Tors and Golden Clough, returning to Fieldhead for five o'clock. A new member of the team doesn't understand one of Malcolm's abbreviations: '7-min crossing.' He explains it is rambler's shorthand for the quickest possible crossing of the five-square-mile Kinder plateau, between Mill Brook and Blackden Brook. 'You take the third grough to the east of Blackden Brook,' he says with a wisdom accumulated over many years of 'bog-trotting'.

Walkers are usually amiable, but for this school party the chat is informative as well as friendly

Ian, a full-time ranger for 16 years, explains there is an extra task for the Patrol Rangers today. They are engaged on a survey for the Park's consultant ecologist, which involves checking the effect walkers have on moorland vegetation. Each ranger is handed a map showing key points where he must stop, look around and count the number of walkers he can see in a particular area. 'Naturalists are concerned at the disturbance to wildlife which large numbers of walkers might be causing in moorland areas,' Ian says. 'We are also interested in finding out exactly where people go on the moorlands, to establish patterns of use.' The Peak National Park has 76 square miles of access land on the northern and eastern moors, where special

agreements drawn up with the owners allow free access to walkers, subject to a commonsense set of bye-laws and closure for a few days each year during the grouse-shooting season (12 August to 10 December).

A thorough briefing session prepares Rangers for the prevailing problems and conditions 'on the hill'

The Peak Park's Ranger Service was set up one cold and wet Good Friday at a meeting outside the Nag's Head pub at Edale in 1954. This was the first ranger service to be operated in a British National Park, and its prime function was to patrol the newly-created access areas. In those days, the warden service – as it was known then – only covered the access areas, an important condition of the agreements. However, after local government reorganisation in 1974 it was expanded to cover the whole of the National Park.

Helping hands

There are four District Rangers, a dozen Area Rangers, and eight Seasonal Rangers on the full-time staff. They are backed up by about 170 part-timers and 200 volunteers, such as those assembled at Fieldhead. The Peak Park Conservation Volunteers are also part of the Ranger Service, and currently perform annually about 3,000 man-days of often back-breaking tasks. Ian's first job that day was to check on a group of volunteers at work in the delightfully-named Golden Clough, just up the Grindsbrook Valley from Edale.

As the others set off on their individual patrols, we walked up past the Nag's Head, a ramblers' pub since the days of 'Bloody Bill the Bog-trotter' – legendary landlord Fred Heardman, who set up the first informal National Park information centre in the snug. Just as we turn off the road to cross the Grinds Brook, an estate car pulls up. It is Bob Townsend, local tenant farmer and chairman of Edale Parish Council. Ian pauses to pass the time of day with him, and reflects on the unseasonably cold weather. Liaison with local people is just as important to the Ranger Service as helping visitors, for potential problems – such as a stray dog worrying sheep or a damaged stile or sign – can usually be solved by a friendly chat.

We said cheerio to Bob and set off over the famous Log Bridge, which is the start of a journey of a lifetime for thousands of ramblers as they embark on Tom Stephenson's epic 250-mile Pennine Way. As we stepped on to the bridge, Ian paused and turned to lift what appeared to be a loose board. Underneath he revealed a pressure-counting device which, even at that early hour, had recorded the passage of nearly 50 walkers. Over the bridge, we climbed a rustic staircase which by-passes the original route of the Pennine Way, fenced off several years ago to halt the erosion caused by thousands of pairs of vibram-soled walking boots. The area is now green again, and sapling trees are thriving. 'Human erosion is a big problem in popular areas like Grindsbrook,' explains Ian. 'We do what we can to try to repair badly-eroded areas and enhance the landscape.'

A few yards up the meadow beneath The Nab we came across a length of rough gritstone cobbles, where the Way had been experimentally paved for a short stretch. It gave easy, dry walking for a few yards, whereas on either side the footpath has been worn into four, five or even six muddy lanes – the infamous 'Pennine Motorway'. 'If we had the manpower and resources, I'd like to provide this sort of well-drained paved surface over all the most badly-eroded sections in lowland situations like this,' says Ian.

Making good

Passing through a scraggy plantation of trees, we came to the kissing gate leading down to Golden Clough. The band of workers from the Derbyshire Conservation Volunteers, based in Derby, were hard at work reconstructing the footpath and drystone wall alongside the bubbling waters. It was a grand setting, with the sharply-pointed peak of Ringing Roger looking like a miniature Matterhorn at the head of the cascading clough. The volunteers were being supervised by Jeremy Brown, Seasonal Ranger and volunteers' organiser. He and Ian discussed progress. The long length of gritstone wall which led down the valley was in a sad state of repair, and the young volunteers were engaged on intricate and laborious reconstruction.

There was some discussion on whether the wall should be 'battered,' that is, smoothly-sloped down following the contours of the clough, or stepped. Ian surveyed the scene. 'We don't expect contractor's standards of walling from volunteers, but we must try to get the best job we can. It is often a case of horses for courses, and we try to match people to the kind of jobs they can do. There's no doubt that if it wasn't for the volunteers, many jobs just wouldn't get done at all. The bonus is that the youngsters from the surrounding cities and towns who come out in these work parties are learning a lot about the countryside and countryside skills.' Other volunteers are wielding picks and shovels, and clearing the ground for an improved set of steps up from the clough and its wooden bridge where the Pennine Way starts its long climb into the Grindsbrook Gorge, towards Kinder Scout. A huge flat boulder from higher up at 'Bungalow Corner' was transported down, balanced precariously on a wheelbarrow, surrounded by willing hands. It will end up as one of the Golden Clough steps.

The day, which had started out bright and sunny, had now deteriorated and the 'clag' (as the mist and clouds are known here) had descended over the head of the valley. Kinder had been beheaded by shifting mist carrying a fine, penetrating rain. It was turning into a typical Kinder day, and those who were tempted by that early-morning sun to head for the heights would now be enveloped. The mountain was showing its other, malevolent face, always ready to catch out the unprepared.

Ian Hurst's district covers about 150 square miles of these brooding, desolate moors, from Castleton in the south to Marsden in the north. He is constantly on call as a mountain-rescue controller, and the base at Fieldhead which we left that morning doubles as a mountain-rescue post. 'We get an average of about one call-out a week,' says Ian. 'Many of our Rangers are members of the local mountain-rescue teams, and as co-ordinator I have to liaise closely with the police and the other emergency services.' His radio call-sign, 'Peakland India' has been busy on the rescue frequencies during the past year, after a severe winter which stretched physical and material resources to the limit. A group of girls on a Duke of Edinburgh Award expedition went missing on the bleak Howden Moors, and a huge sweep search was instituted, involving two helicopters. Fortunately, they were found – lost, but safe and well. Ian also had to evacuate a young lad off the dangerous face of the so-called 'Shivering Mountain' of Mam Tor, near Castleton, after he had ventured too far on to its shifting shales. Ian has done some climbing, but does not regard himself as an expert.

Anyone who has experienced the isolation of the high moors will appreciate why radio links are a must

It is not only people who have to be rescued. A couple of years ago the Rangers were involved in an extraordinary series of rescues when Ian was stationed in the West and Central District. On successive weeks, he was called on to retrieve sheep from a ledge on a vertical limestone cliff in Water-cum-Jolly Dale, above the rushing waters of the River Wye. On both occasions the sheep had strayed and slipped down on to the ledge, from which there was no way back. 'The funny thing was, we think it was the same sheep both times,' recalled Ian, who received an RSPCA commendation for his action in retrieving the animal. It was sheep again, during the last bitter winter, which had to be rescued as they became buried by the score in mountainous snowdrifts whipped up by the biting winds. The Park's Ranger Service was praised by police and farmers alike for the Herculean efforts they put in to assist both man and beast in the atrocious conditions. Many sheep died, but many others were saved as they were dug out or fed by teams of Rangers working round the clock.

It is not only in winter that the emergency service provided by the Rangers is called on. High summer can be a time of severe pressure too, when the peat-covered moors can quickly turn as dry as the proverbial tinder box. A carelessly-discarded match, cigarette end or even broken glass is enough to ignite the peat into a raging fire which, because of the nature of the material, can burn for weeks. Ian recalled the aerial fire-spotting exercise he was involved in during the dry summer of 1980. 'As we flew over the area, it looked as if the whole place was going to go up in flames.' Fire-fighting on a peat moor is a thankless task. Surprisingly, a moor which is a waterlogged bog in the winter can turn into a dust-ridden desert after a spell of hot, dry weather, and water is often a long way from the seat of the fire. Five-gallon backpacks weighing 50lbs or more are used to carry water and a herbicide-type spray nozzle to the fire, and it is usually a long, hot and dusty walk to the nearest hillside spring. Nowadays, the service also has the multi-purpose Argocat vehicle to help transport water and men to the scene of a fire. This eight-wheeled, go-anywhere vehicle has greatly assisted in the logistical problems in both summer and winter – when fodder was taken to stock – but the Rangers only have one.

Long commitment

Ian has a strong sympathy for the farming community, for after he left school in Sheffield he spent some time in working on local farms in the Bradfield area. His introduction to the Ranger Service was as a young lad of 15 or 16, when he saw a man wearing the distinctive armband while he was out walking near Kinder Downfall – the spectacular waterfall which gave Kinder Scout its name. 'I saw this chap representing the National Park – and I have a strong suspicion it was Malcolm Padley – and I thought to myself, I'd like

to do that.' He took his warden training-course certificate in 1963 and became a Patrol Warden at the age of 21, based at Stanage on the Eastern Edges. Later, he became a full-timer and moved to Crowden-in-Longdendale in 1970 as an assistant warden. Such is the attraction of a Ranger's outdoor life that when Ian left Crowden on promotion as District Ranger for the West and Central District in 1977, there were over 1,000 applications for his job, from clergymen to high-flying young executives. Ian knows he is in a job which is the envy of many, although he is equally sure that if they knew the salary and the unsociable hours which he has to put in, many would also have second thoughts at the prospect.

'I thoroughly enjoy the life,' confessed Ian as we headed back down to Edale in the steady drizzle. 'But like any other job, it has its good and bad sides. For most visitors and local people we *are* the National Park, for we are likely to be the only representatives they meet in the field. Therefore we have to be Rangers, ready to solve little local problems; information officers, helping and directing visitors, and sometimes even the link with the planners back at the Park headquarters.

'I never try to force myself on people, although most folk on the hill will want to speak as you pass. We are there to give help if required, but we are not there to impose ourselves or the authority on people, most of whom are either out just to enjoy this marvellous scenery, or getting on with their own lives as farmers or local residents.'

A message on the wall of the Fieldhead briefing centre from 'a satisfied customer' puts it succinctly: 'Above 2,000ft, the most comprehensive social service in the country.'

No matter how good they are with maps and compass, walkers are always comforted by the waymarks sited even in remote places by the National Park Rangers

PEAK DISTRICT

Gazetteer

Each entry in this Gazetteer has the atlas
page number on which the place can be
found and its National Grid reference
included under the heading.
An explanation of how to use the National
Grid is given on page 78.

*Above: cable cars leave for the Heights of Abraham just
upstream of Matlock Bath railway station*

Alstonefield

Map Ref: 94SK1355

Alstonefield stands at 900ft between the Dove and Manifold, and 150 years ago was a huge parish embracing all the land between the two rivers. Although much reduced it still remains large, and includes the hamlet of Milldale – at the northern end of Dovedale – among other scattered settlements. Its site is at the junction of several ancient tracks, later to become packhorse ways, and in 1308 it received a charter for the market that continued there until 1500. Annual cattle sales were held in the yard of the George Inn right up until early this century.

Spurned by canal and railway engineers for sound geographical reasons, Alstonefield lies some 2 miles from the nearest classified road and is today a charmingly unspoiled village. Several of its mullioned-windowed houses form a delightful group with the George around the village green, between which and the church is the Hall – formerly the Rectory – of 1587. Behind this is a tithe barn, featuring an internal wall of exposed wattle and daub and a spiral stone staircase, which may have belonged to its predecessor.

There has been a church at Alstonefield since at least 892, but the earliest parts of the present building – the Norman south doorway and chancel arch – date from around 1100. The remainder is a mixture of the Decorated and Perpendicular styles, with a profusion of 17th-century woodwork including box pews and a two-decker pulpit of 1637. Both features were by a local man called Edward Unsworth.

The elaborate grey-green pew belonged to the Cottons of Beresford Hall – birthplace of Izaak Walton's friend Charles Cotton, who wrote the second part of *The Compleat Angler*. Although the Hall was demolished in 1858, the fishing temple built by Cotton to entertain Walton survives on private ground in Beresford Dale.

AA recommends:
Self Catering: ◇ Alders & Corner Cottage, *tel.* (033527) 201 ◇ Rose Cottage, Riverside, *tel.* (033529) 447

Arbor Low

Map Ref: 92SK1663

Having walked through a farmyard and up a sloping field to reach the Peak's largest stone circle, the visitor may be momentarily disappointed to find that the 47 perimeter and three central stones are all recumbent. However, the fascination of this impressive monument from the late Neolithic and early Bronze Age period –

Arbor Low is a henge monument with lying rather than standing stones

around 2,000BC – quickly exerts its undeniable presence.

It has the usual henge features – a 250ft-diameter circular bank and 30ft-wide ditch, with two entrance causeways across them. At the centre of this enclosure is the 150ft-diameter circle of stones, near the middle of which excavations in 1902 discovered remains of a man who had been buried without the grave goods that would normally have been included to ease his transition into the next world. Relics found in an early Bronze Age barrow on the bank include a stone cist, or small burial chamber containing cremations, a bone pin and two food vessels.

A contemporary linear earthwork is visible for about 200yds south of Arbor Low, while some 350yds south west of this feature on 1,150ft Gib Hill is Peakland's largest round barrow. Excavations near its top in 1848 revealed a cist containing a cremation and a food vessel. Earlier burials may be waiting for discovery a little deeper down.

Ashbourne

Map Ref: 80SK1846

Although this attractive little market town straggles along Henmore Brook a mile or so south of the National Park boundary, it is a good centre from which to explore the valleys of the Dove and Manifold – and indeed, the whole south-western corner of the Peak. In a sense it is a frontier town between lowland Britain to the south and the more rugged landscape of highland Britain in the north. Most of its buildings are of typical Midland red brick, but a sprinkling of stone reminds the visitor of the Peak's proximity.

The *Esseburne* of *Domesday* was a small settlement sited north of the Henmore, around an already ancient church. Immediately to the east, a 13th-century lord of the manor laid out a new town with a long main street, large triangular market place and parallel building plots – or 'burgages' – stretching to back lanes. He obtained a market charter in 1257.

To avoid paying the town's tolls while enjoying its benefits, some traders built themselves houses south of the brook in what became the suburb of Compton, which was eventually absorbed into the town.

Ashbourne developed slowly until the 18th-century coaching heyday, when it became a fashionable social centre. Many of its best buildings were built or refaced in that Georgian era, some of the finest of which are seen in Church Street and St John Street.

At the western end of this 'double' street is the splendid cruciform parish church of St Oswald, described by George Eliot as the 'finest mere parish church in England'. Capped by the tallest spire (212ft) around the Peak District, it contains Thomas Banks' famous monument in Carrara marble to Penelope Boothby, who died aged five in 1793.

Also at the western end of the street is The Mansion, a late 17th-century house refaced in the 1760s for Dr Johnson's oldest friend, the Reverend Dr John Taylor. Dr Taylor lived there in considerable style on an income derived from various benefices which he rarely visited. Almost opposite is The Grey House, which has a finer Georgian frontage and belonged to an innkeeper who eventually owned the Buxton baths. Next door is the original stone-built Grammar School – founded by Queen Elizabeth I in 1585, completed by 1606 and visited by Queen Elizabeth II on the occasion of its quatercentenary.

Spanning St John Street is the rare 'gallows' inn-sign of the Green Man and Black's Head Royal Hotel, a name commemorating the amalgamation of two coaching inns in 1825. James Boswell found the Green Man 'a very good inn' and its landlady 'a mighty civil gentlewoman'. A recently restored timber-framed shop close by makes the traditional Ashbourne gingerbread, reputedly to a recipe acquired from French prisoners detained in Ashbourne during the Napoleonic Wars.

A better known Ashbourne tradition is the annual football game played through the streets and along the Henmore on Shrove Tuesday and Ash Wednesday between teams of no set number, nominally representing the 'Up'ards' and the 'Down'ards' – the brook being the dividing line. Its history, like its rules and skills, has long been forgotten; but it is great fun (except perhaps for property owners), and numerous attempts to ban it have all been rightly thwarted.

AA recommends:
Campsite: Sandybrook Hall Holiday Centre, 3-pennants, *tel.* (0335) 42679

Ashford in the Water

Map Ref: 92SK1969

On occasion this delightful place name has been all too accurate, but normally the pellucid waters of the trout-filled River Wye keep to the their channel between the houses, and away from the bypass which takes the A6 round the elegant village itself.

'Sheepwash' is the oldest, narrowest and most picturesque of several bridges spanning the Wye here. Originally for pack-horses but now closed to all traffic, it takes its name from an adjacent stone enclosure in which sheep used to be washed – and occasionally still are, for demonstration purposes.

A virgin crant, or garland, hanging in the church roof at Ashford in the Water

Holy Trinity Church preserves four white paper garlands, or 'virgin crants', which used to be carried at the funerals of unmarried girls.

Ashford, which dresses six wells, has numerous 18th-century buildings and a few from the 17th – including a tithe barn now serving as an art gallery, and the largely unspoilt Devonshire Arms.

AA recommends:
Campsite: ◇ Greenhills Caravan Park, Crow Hill Ln, 3-pennants, *tel.* (062981) 2467 & 3052

Underground Riches

Many of the thousands of tourists who flock to Castleton annually come away with souvenirs made from a unique mineral found in the hills surrounding the little township at the head of the Hope Valley.

The beautiful blue, purple, yellow and white-banded fluorspar known as Blue John is a Castleton speciality, found only in Treak Cliff – the limestone hill which stands between the village and Mam Tor. It was formed millions of years ago when waves of hot minerals from the earth's core surged up between cracks and fissures in the limestone which, in places like Treak Cliff, was impregnated by natural oils or hydrocarbons. When these molten solutions cooled, they were transformed into the banded crystals of fluorspar.

The name is thought to come from the French *bleu-jaune* meaning 'blue-yellow', or it may have been adopted by the early lead miners to differentiate it from 'black-jack', their name for zinc-blende.

There is a persistent local legend that Blue John was first worked by the Romans, but this is perhaps based on the fact that two vases made of similar fluorspar were unearthed during the excavations at Pompeii. There is no real evidence that they came from Castleton.

The first accurate record of Blue John was not made until the late 17th century. From the middle of the 18th century the Midland engineer Matthew Boulton used Blue John as a foil for the ormolu (gilded bronze) in the ornaments he created for many stately homes. Later, Robert Adam used it as an inlay for fireplaces at Kedleston Hall, near Derby. In 1768 Boulton unsuccessfully tried to obtain a monopoly of the Blue John mines, which at their height produced 20 tons annually.

Blue John, a decorative mineral that is found in caves and mines near Castleton

Today that figure is down to only about half a ton, and the mineral is found in veins averaging three inches in thickness – making it only suitable for jewellery and small ornaments. Visitors can still see veins of Blue John, of which 14 types are recognised, in the Blue John and Treak Cliff Caverns. The best of the Treak Cliff chambers were accidentally discovered in 1926, when miners searching for Blue John blasted their way into the beautifully-decorated inner caverns.

Another bituminous impurity in the limestone created Ashford Black Marble, which was in much demand during Victorian times as a material for *objets d'art*. Really a compact and finely-textured grey limestone, the 'marble' is created by fine polishing of the cut surface, which gives it a brilliant, satin-black appearance.

Black marble from the mines in the Ashford in the Water district was used for clock cases, candlesticks, book-ends, inkstands and miniature obelisks. It was also sought after for intricate inlays in table tops, murals and fireplaces in the homes of the well-to-do, including Hardwick Hall and Chatsworth.

Unlike Blue John, Ashford Black Marble has a record of human exploitation which goes back into prehistory, for pieces of dressed marble have been found in burial mounds near by.

A White Peak panorama stretching across the rolling Derbyshire hills from the 1,807ft watershed of Axe Edge

Ashover

Map Ref: 81SK3463

This sprawling collection of scattered settlements covers almost 10,000 acres and is a place of charm and quirky character, built almost entirely of stone quarried from hills within the parish. Exploration should begin in the main village, where the church interior is as rewarding as the setting and its 15th-century tower and spire suggest. In particular, the alabaster tomb-chest with effigies of Thomas Babington (died 1518) and his wife has been called 'the best in Derbyshire'. Surprisingly, the Norman font is the only lead one in a lead-producing county of which Ashover was a centre. The association is obvious from the memorials on the walls – note especially the one in 'Memory of David Wall, whose superior performance on the Bassoon endeared him to an extensive musical acquaintance. . . .'

Next to the church is the Crispin Inn, which claims (dubiously) to date from 1416 – the Agincourt year. It more likely dates, like many other buildings in the parish, from the 17th century. The whole village is worth exploring, and in places it is possible to follow the track of the Ashover Light Railway. This friendly little line was built to take lime from Ashover to Clay Cross Works, but between 1925 and 1959 provided a passenger service between the village and the main line at Stretton.

Surrounding hills – especially High Ordish or Cocking Tor – provide splendid views over Ashover and along the valley of the River Amber, on the banks of which the village stands.

Axe Edge

Map Ref: 91SK0370

This long, gritstone escarpment rises to 1,807ft and is one of Peakland's grandest viewpoints. The A53 Buxton-Leek road following its eastern flank offers a spectacular drive – while the A54 Buxton to Congleton highway to the west is scarcely less dramatic. Axe Edge Moor, which lies between the two, is strictly for hardy walkers. It receives over 50 inches of rain annually, and the snow often lingers long into spring.

Not surprisingly, it is a watershed and the source of five important rivers. The Dove and Manifold rise close together just east of the A53, and after following almost parallel courses join forces at Ilam to flow south-eastward into the Trent and thence the North Sea. About two miles north, the Wye rises above Buxton to run south into the Derwent and eventually the Trent. The Goyt, however, rises just west of the Edge and flows north to become one of the main sources of the Mersey. There it is joined by

Oddly, the Norman lead font at Ashover is unique in a former lead-mining area

the Dane, which has run south and then west around the Cheshire Plain from a source less than two miles from the head of the Goyt.

Close to the Goyt's source on the A537 Buxton-Macclesfield road is the solitary Cat and Fiddle Inn, which at 1,690ft is the second highest inn in England – after Tan Hill Inn between Swaledale and Teesdale. On the Leek road are the Traveller's Rest at just over 1,500ft, and the Royal Cottage, just below 1,500ft.

Between the two is a minor road leading to Flash, which at 1,518ft proclaims itself to be England's highest village. That may make St Paul's Church (built 1744, rebuilt 1901) the highest parish church – in a non-doctrinal sense. A gang of coiners once operated in this remote spot, hence the term 'flash' for counterfeit money.

AA recommends:
Self Catering: ◇ Northfield Farm (Old Stables), Flash, *tel.* (0298) 2543

almsmen below, until the row of almshouses behind was added in 1709. Bakewell is full of good old buildings deserving of inspection. Many date from around 1700 when the Duke of Rutland was trying to establish a spa – unsuccessfully, because the water was colder than at Buxton. The Bath House of 1697 and Bath Gardens survive from that time.

Along the A6 on the town's northern edge, close to Arkwright's Lumford Mill (established 1777), a typically low-parapeted packhorse bridge of 1664 spans the River Wye. The town bridge is more than 300 years older. Rainbow trout and ducks queue up to be fed by the riverside walk below.

AA recommends:

Hotels: Croft Country House, Gt Longstone, 2-star country house hotel, *tel.* (062987) 278
Millford House, Mill St, 2-star, *tel.* (0629) 812130
Restaurant: ◇ Fischers, Woodhouse, Bath St, 1-fork rosette, *tel.* (0629) 812687
Campsite: Haddon Grove Farm, Haddon Grove, Over Haddon, Venture site, *tel.* (062981) 2343 (3m W off B5055)
Guesthouses: Cliffe House Hotel, Monsal Head, *tel.* (062987) 376
Merlin House Country Hotel, Ashford Ln, Monsal Head, *tel.* (062987) 475

Bakewell church is a delightful pot-pourri of architectural styles and periods

Bakewell

Map Ref: 92SK2168

Bakewell has Derbyshire's second busiest livestock market and the headquarters of the Peak Park Joint Planning Board. The Board's Information Centre is housed in a splendid, converted 17th-century market hall in the town centre, where Bridge Street meets the attractive Market Place.

Badecean Wiellon ('Beadeca's spring'), as the *Anglo-Saxon Chronicle* called it, sprang up at a natural crossing-point of the Wye – once guarded by a castle built by Edward the Elder in 942. Already a sizable royal manor by the time of the *Domesday* survey, it had a market, which was confirmed by a charter in 1330 and banished from the streets to its present site in 1826.

In 1086 Bakewell, at the centre of a vast ecclesiastical parish, was the only place in the area with two priests. Traces of the Saxon church remain, as do the well-preserved stumps of two Saxon crosses in the hillside churchyard, and fragments of others in the south porch. The tower and spire that dominate the town are mainly a 19th-century rebuild, the rest of the church being an intricate mixture of all periods from the 12th century onwards. The various works are extremely well labelled and interpreted for the benefit of visitors. Not to be missed are the monuments in the Vernon chapel, including that of Dorothy Vernon and her husband John Manners (see Haddon Hall).

That applies equally to the Old House Museum farther up the hill in Cunningham Place. As interesting as the admirable local folk collection is the early-Tudor house itself, and the story of its restoration after rescue from imminent demolition.

Probably equally old are the houses of Avenel Court, below the church in King Street, though they are disguised behind a 1780 shop front. In the same square is the old Town Hall of 1684. Originally the upper floor only was used, with

Bakewell Puddings

If you don't want to upset the locals in Bakewell, just be careful how you refer to their most famous homemade delicacy. Mr Kipling may call his version 'tarts', but you'll get some black looks if you ask for them by that name in the town of their origin. In Bakewell they are *always* known as 'puddings' which is, in any case, a more accurate description of this unique sweet which now carries the name of the Peakland 'capital' all over the world.

The story of the Bakewell Pudding is one of a disaster which turned into a delicacy. According to tradition, the first Bakewell Pudding was created by mistake by a flustered cook at the former White Horse Inn, in Matlock Street, around 1860.

Mrs Greaves, the landlady of the inn, issued instructions for her cook to prepare a strawberry tart for some important guests. The cook, in the hustle of a busy kitchen, mistakenly put the jam in first and then poured in the egg mixture designed for the pastry on top. The resulting sweet-tasting pudding, far from being a disaster, was voted an instant hit by the distinguished guests and became a regular item on the inn's menu by popular demand.

When the cook, whose name unfortunately has been lost to posterity, made her will, she wrote down the fortuitous recipe. Who was left with the original, 'real' version of the instructions is still a matter for local dispute and rivalry, for two local bakeries which make puddings claim the privilege.

The Old Original Pudding Shop in Bridge Street was built in the late 17th century and, despite the name, started life as a chandler's shop making candles. Mrs Wilson, the wife of the chandler, is said to have first seen the commercial possibilities of the puddings, and obtained the recipe. The other claimant is the bakery in Matlock Street, which was said to have been given the recipe by the man who helped the cook write her will.

However, the actual mixture remains a closely-guarded secret, although the ingredients are fairly common knowledge: eggs, butter, strawberry jam, flaky pastry and a hint of almond essence. The result, a fairly ordinary-looking dish, is now taken all over the world by tourists who visit the pretty market town by the Wye – and some puddings are even sent by post!

Local claimants to Bakewell's first pudding recipe produce delicious results

Bamford

Map Ref: 88SK2083

Although its railway station is on the Hope Valley line, Bamford village lies farther north up the Derwent, clinging to the steep lower slopes of Bamford Edge above the river. A cotton mill established there around 1780 burnt down within a decade – like so many others, and was rebuilt in 1791. After closure in 1965 it was turned to the production of electric furnaces. William Butterfield designed the church, with its unusual tower and spire, when Bamford became an independent parish in 1860.

A hill-farming village, Bamford is well-known for its annual sheep dog trials on the late spring bank holiday. It is also noted for its popular inns, and its position as the last village south of the spectacular Derwent reservoirs.

Immediately west of Ashopton Viaduct a good, unclassified road runs up to the head of Howden, but at busy times there are restrictions on motorists beyond the Fairholmes parking area and information point, as in the Goyt Valley. Cycles may be hired there.

Dr Barnes Wallis used the awe-inspiring Derwent Dam for his 'bouncing bomb' experiments during the hostile interlude of World War II, and much of *The Dambusters* was filmed on its wide waters.

AA recommends:
Hotels: Marquis of Granby, Hathersage Rd, 2-star, *tel.* (0433) 51206
Rising Sun, Castleton Rd, 2-star, *tel.* (0433) 51323

Baslow

Map Ref: 93SK2572

South from the Hope Valley runs the escarpment of the East Moors in a continuous series of razor-sharp 'edges', jagged with boulders, to form a natural eastern wall to the Derwent Valley. At the northern end of stately Chatsworth Park, where the valley widens slightly to receive Bar Brook, is Baslow village. This is divided into three distinct settlements and sits prettily between the ridge and Derwent River.

At Nether End is the private, north entrance to the park, with lodges by Wyatville (1840) and several hotels. Bridge End has a broach-spired church on the river bank. Its tower clock displays the name *'Victoria'* and the date '1897' instead of numerals, an idea of the local Dr Wrench. A whip inside the church was once used by an official to drive out stray dogs during services. Close by is a 17th-century three-arched bridge, and a tiny tollhouse with a doorway 3½ft high – probably reduced when the level of the road was raised.

On Baslow Edge stands a Wellington Monument erected by Dr Wrench in 1866, balancing a Nelson Monument on Birchen Edge a mile away. The A621 Sheffield road passes between them beyond Far End as it climbs to the exhilarating desolation of Big Moor and Ramsley Moor.

AA recommends:
Hotel: Cavendish, 3-star (red), *tel.* (024688) 2311

Time for memories at Baslow's church

Baslow Edge marks the change from jagged gritstone moors to the softer, pastoral aspect of limestone countryside

Sunshine enhances rather than dispels the brooding quality of Beeley Moor

Beeley

Map Ref: 93SK2667

Beeley, an estate village at the south end of Chatsworth Park, is missed by most tourists because its main street lies east of the Chatsworth road. Much of it was laid out by Paxton for the 6th Duke of Devonshire, rather in the style of Edensor village (see Chatsworth), but some buildings are older – including the early 17th-century Old Hall and the nucleus of the Devonshire Arms.

Beside the inn a minor road climbs to heather-clad Beeley Moor (1,200ft), where there are more than 30 prehistoric barrows and cairns. Hob Hurst's house, the traditional home of the goblin Hob Hurst, is a Bronze Age barrow which lies within a ditch and bank high on Harland Edge.

The numerous steep-sided narrow gullies criss-crossing the peat moors are hereabouts called 'sicks'.

Birchover

Map Ref: 93SK2462

In Birchover the village street climbs gently to Stanton Moor, the source of pinkish warm stone of which its houses were built 'by instalments, and with little regard to regularity', according to a visitor in 1848.

Those instalments have taken place over a period of 300 years,

but the vernacular style in the Peak has changed so little over the period that the houses blend together perfectly. The irregularity of siting, common among Peak villages, is caused by a shortage of level ground on which to build.

The two hospitable village inns were probably among the early 'instalments', with the Red Lion having grown over three centuries from a single 'houseplace' with a 30ft well, now under thick glass just inside the entrance. The Druid Inn, noted for its bar food, used to supply a guide to escort visitors over nearby Rowtor Rocks – a somewhat superfluous exercise since the gritstone assembly rises to no more than 150ft and extends for a mere 80yds. Dimensions aside, it is as impressive as it is surprising, and despite legends of druidical origins it is actually the remains of an otherwise eroded ridge.

The caves and seats on Rowtor were carved out by an eccentric clergyman, the Reverend Thomas Eyre, who died in 1717. He liked to sit on the rocks composing sermons for delivery in the little chapel below – where nowadays can be seen extraordinary wood carvings, primitive wall paintings and a war memorial pulpit (1949) that were the work of a modern and equally creative incumbent.

Bonsall

Map Ref: 93SK2858

This hillside village is just as irregular and engaging as Birchover, the major difference being that it is built of an almost white local limestone and features gritstone mullions, door-jambs and lintels. Roofs are of stone slate.

From the Pig of Lead inn the village street climbs 450ft to Upper Town, which is 850ft above sea level and just below the rim of the limestone plateau. Halfway up is a tiny market place, with a medieval stone cross on a circular base of 13 steps. Its shaft was renewed in 1871. Overlooking it is the King's Head, established in 1677 by Anthony Abell, and close by in High Street is the roughly contemporary manor house. Even the parish church is on split levels, which makes it accessible only by numerous steps.

Bonsall was once a stocking-making village, and one or two tiny workshops remain amongst the pigeon lofts. It was even more a lead-mining centre and the plateau is a honeycomb of miners' tracks and mine shafts. Most of the excavations have been capped, but care is still needed by anyone walking there – perhaps searching for the source of the little Bonsall Brook, which dictated the shape of the village and turned the wheels of many mills in Bonsall and along the tree-lined Via Gellia valley road to Cromford. Features of that interesting village include Arkwright's mill and the original Viyella mill – which took its name from the Via Gellia, built in the 1790s by Philip Gell of Hopton Hall for the carriage of lead and stones from his mines and quarries to the Cromford Canal terminus.

Bonsall's tiny market place features an attractive medieval stone cross mounted on a circular dais comprising 13 steps

Bradfield

Map Ref: 85SK2692

From the A57 Snake Pass road, the first (or last) northward unclassified lane east of Ashopton Viaduct leads over an enchanted countryside of wild moorland and deep, green valleys to the village of Bradfield. On the way it passes the reputedly 14th-century Strines Inn and runs close to the expansive Strines and Dale Dike reservoirs.

Both the feel of the country and the architecture of the rare buildings are different from those of the Derbyshire and Staffordshire Peak. If any more confirmation is needed, the superb cricket ground round which Low Bradfield seems to have built confirms that this is Yorkshire.

Bradfield is sited at 860ft in a sheltering fold of high moorland above the Loxley Valley, nestling tightly round a splendid castellated, pinnacled and much-gargoyled church in a situation that would seem utterly remote but for urban-type bus-stop signs which remind visitors that the urban sprawl of Sheffield is just 7 miles away.

A mere chapel-of-ease until 1868, St Nicholas is among the largest and grandest Peakland village churches, owing its opulence to Ecclesfield Priory – who built it and provided its early priests. Dating chiefly from the late 15th century, it has a 14th-century tower and preserves fragments of Norman work from an earlier building. Superb views from its south porch span the valley and the Agden and Damflask reservoirs to the moors beyond – but the eye is also attracted downward to a patchwork of walled fields in a wide bowl that would be the original broad-field (or fold) that features in the place name.

The Watch House, an oddly-shaped Gothic private house was built in 1745 for guarding against body snatchers who might be intent on plundering the adjoining churchyard. The village stocks and a double horse trough are near by, while at the edge of a wood west of the church are traces of a motte-and-bailey castle. Another motte can be seen farther east.

Sheffield Viking Sailing Club has its headquarters on Damflask Reservoir, which is also a popular picnicking spot.

AA recommends:
Campsite: Strangers Home Inn, The Street, 1-pennant, *tel.* (0255) 87304

Bradwell

Map Ref: 88SK1781

Sandwiched by towering cliffs between Hope Valley and Bradwell Dale, Bradwell is a place with lots of character and an industrial tradition. In addition to pursuing the usual Peakland extractive industries it has made lead miners' hard hats – known as 'Bradders beavers' – coarse-cotton goods, opera glasses, telescopes and umbrellas. It now has a vast cement works on its north-western edge and is a producer of excellent home-made ice-cream.

For the industrial archaeologist Bradwell's attractions are obvious, but the lay tourist makes for Bagshawe Cavern, which was discovered by lead miners in 1806 and is reached by descending 130 steps. The 'jitties' or 'ginnels', narrow passageways off the 'main road', are worth exploring.

One mile south is Hazlebadge Hall, a former manor house (now a farm) dating from 1549. Brough, the same distance north, is a hamlet with a water-mill on the site of the Roman fort of *Navio* – of which nothing remains above ground.

Buxton

Map Ref: 91SK0673

A famous annual festival and the restoration of Buxton's main buildings has revived the one-time spa resort after a period of decline that had affected most of its contemporaries during a mid-20th century recession thereabouts.

The Peak Rail Centre, a separate transport museum, and the unique Micrarium – an exhibition of nature under the microscope – are among the new attractions in this tourist and conference centre. Older features that are still popular include Poole's Cavern – reputed home of a medieval outlaw and the undisputed home of man in Romano-British times – and Grin Low Wood, designated a country park. Buxton Hall was rebuilt in 1670 and is now

Buxton Spa

Akinder climate and a few feet lower in altitude, and Buxton might have become a spa to rival Bath or Cheltenham.

However, the climatic disadvantages associated with being the highest market town in England meant that the 5th Duke of Devonshire's 'Grand Design' to create a northern Bath was never realised.

Early travellers complained of its 'dreary hills', its 'dismal situation' and the fact it was 'liable to incessant rains from the height of the surrounding hills'.

The 1,000ft altitude was not enough to deter the spa-seeking Romans, however, who called their settlement *Aqua Arnemetiae*, which has been translated as 'the spa of the goddess of the grove'.

It was the constant 82 degrees F (28 degrees C) temperature of the pale blue, slightly effervescent waters from the eight thermal springs which attracted the Romans. Later, their apparently miraculous health-giving properties made them extremely popular with pilgrims, to the extent that Henry VIII ordered them to be closed.

By the time of Elizabeth I, the wells were again attracting so many that no 'dyseased or ympotent poore person living on Almes' was allowed in, unless they had a licence from two Justices. Mary Queen of Scots, detained for so many years at Sheffield and Chatsworth, was a frequent visitor who 'took the waters' for her chronic rheumatism, and wrote gratefully after her first visit: 'I have not been at all disappointed, thank God.'

The profits made from his copper mines at Ecton Hill in Staffordshire encouraged the 5th Duke of Devonshire to develop the lofty hill town into a spa. He appointed the architect John Carr of York to design the splendid Crescent on the model of John Wood's Royal Crescent at Bath. The total cost of the superb, Doric-style building – which originally housed three hotels – was £120,000. It was finished in 1784.

The natural baths and St Ann's Well were also improved at this time, and in 1790, on the slope behind The Crescent, the Great Stables and Riding School were constructed to house the hotel visitors' horses. In 1858 the 6th Duke converted this building into a hospital, and in 1880 the circular central courtyard was enclosed in what is still the largest unsupported dome in the world, with a span of 154ft.

By the time of the 6th Duke Buxton had developed into a

the Old Hall Hotel, probably the oldest building in a Georgian and mid-Victorian town.

Calver

Map Ref: 89SK2474

Stone-built Calver stands on the River Derwent, which is spanned here by a good 18th-century bridge now bypassed by a new structure carrying the main A623. Both are overlooked by an austerely handsome Georgian cotton mill – now used for other industrial purposes – which keen television addicts with long memories may recognise as Colditz Castle in the TV series, *Colditz*. A road heading past the mill from east of the bridge and through the village of Curbar on to Curbar Edge passes – at the top edge of the village – just north of a circular lock-up with conical roof. It is well worth a second glance, as is the view from the nearby National Trust property of Curbar Gap.

Just west of Calver Bridge is a good craft centre, and beyond that the settlement of Calver Sough, which takes its name from the entrance to a drainage 'sough'. There are many such channels in the Peak, laid at enormous expense to free lead mines from water seeping through fissures in the limestone. A right turn by the traffic lights at Calver South leads through Froggatt village and on to Froggatt Edge, where there are 76 acres of National Trust woodland, meadow and pasture.

Both Curbar and Froggatt – nestling below their respective edges – are desirable residential villages much favoured by commuters, who can enjoy splendid walks and superb views along the valley and still be in their Sheffield offices within a comfortable 20 minutes.

Left: Pavilion Gardens in full bloom

Below: Carr's Crescent, now and then

fashionable health resort, and he employed Sir Jeffrey Wyatville to design the elegant parish church, and in 1811 lay out the graded paths of The Slopes.

The long-awaited coming of the railway in 1863 marked the zenith of Buxton's popularity, when the imposing Palace Hotel of 1868, the Pavilion and Pavilion Gardens of 1871 and the ornate Opera House of 1905 – now the home of the international Buxton Festival of Music and the Arts – were built.

The 18th century has been brought back to life in Buxton – as its Opera House shows

Spectacular underground formations are a feature of Treak Cliff Cavern, Castleton

Castleton

Map Ref: 88SK1583

Laid out as a planned town below the dominant Norman castle where Henry II accepted the submission of Malcolm King of Scotland in 1157, Castleton is unchanged in shape but is nowadays a village that has become a highly-popular and thriving tourist centre.

Ruined Peveril Castle, in the care of English Heritage, has an original curtain wall showing early-Norman herring-bone work on the north side – the only flank without natural defences. Henry II built the present keep 19 years after his triumph over Malcolm, and the gatehouse is also of the 12th century. The slightly later hall and circular towers are noteworthy in containing Roman brick, probably from the remains of *Navio*.

Below the castle is the awesome mouth of Peak Cavern, about 50ft high and twice that wide, which once sheltered cottages and still harbours a ropewalk that only recently ceased to be used. From the mouth emerges a tributary of the Derwent, called Peakshole Water. Visitors have been enjoying guided tours of the cave for at least 300 years, which is about as long as the famous Blue John stone – a purplish-blue form of fluorspar – has been commercially extracted from lead workings sited about a mile west below Mam Tor.

The Blue John, Treak Cliff and Speedwell Caverns – all open to the public – are mixtures of natural cavities and lead mine workings, but with displays of stalactites and stalagmites similar to those found in Peak Cavern and other Derbyshire caves. Speedwell differs from the rest in that it is reached by a 104-step descent to a boat which is guided for about half-a-mile along an underground canal to a partly-natural cavern which was also the working face of the former Speedwell Mine. Treak Cliff is virtually the only remaining viable source of Blue John.

St Edmund's Church, though heavily restored in 1837, retains 17th-century box pews, a fine Normal chancel arch, and a valuable library which includes a 1611 'Breeches' Bible. Possibly on a more pagan note, a popular event in the village calendar is the annual Garland Day.

Overlooking Castleton is Mam Tor, also called the 'Shivering Mountain' because layers of soft shale between the harder beds of gritstone are constantly crumbling. From the village its 1,695ft bulk looks like a half-eaten apple, and the Bronze and Iron Age fort on its summit is under threat from erosion. Also, the A625 main road round the foot of the mountain has been permanently closed because of cracks in the surface, with traffic being diverted up the Winnat's Pass. This steep, narrow defile between high limestone cliffs was once a coach road and nowadays carries a Site of Special Scientific Interest designation.

Castleton Hall is a 17th-century house now serving as a Youth Hostel, while the 19th-century Losehill Hall is the Park Board's Residential Study Centre – the first of its kind to be set up by a National Park authority, and possibly the precursor of more.

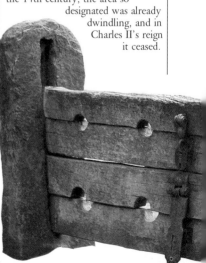

Rugged, dramatic defile of Winnat's Pass

Chapel-en-le-Frith

Map Ref: 87SK0680

As its name suggests, this town was originally a foresters' chapel in the Royal Forest of the High Peak – a huge stretch of wasteland, not necessarily all wooded, reserved as a royal hunting ground.

By the time the present parish church replaced the chapel early in the 14th century, the area so designated was already dwindling, and in Charles II's reign it ceased.

Chapel developed into a market town to which – about the turn of the century – it added vehicle-brake manufacture. This had curious origins in the footwear industry, which gave rise to the term brake 'shoes'. The cobbled market place (760ft above sea level) has a medieval market cross and stocks.

Two miles north-west, sandwiched between the massive bulk of Chinley Churn (1,480ft) and the conical-topped Eccles Pike (1,213ft), is the once-important Chinley railway junction. Although it has lost much of its former status, it has retained two magnificent stone viaducts.

A mile farther west is Buxworth, which is bisected by a bypass road and features numerous relics of an earlier phase of the Industrial Revolution. Included are the terminal canal basin (now being restored), of the Peak Forest Canal – completed in 1800 by Benjamin Outram – and well-preserved remains of his Peak Forest Tramway. Operated partly by gravity, the tramway brought limestone and lime from the quarries and kilns six miles away at Dove Holes.

The village was called Bugsworth until the inhabitants, weary of the jokes, had its name officially changed in 1929. Bugsworth Hall, however, has proudly retained the old spelling, along with its gables and mullions of 1627.

Chatsworth

Map Ref: 93SK2570

'Not so much a house as a town', the Duchess of Devonshire says of Chatsworth, but it is a very beautiful town. The first view of it across the park from the south is unforgettable. In the foreground – across the Derwent – the Emperor fountain sends up a 290ft jet of water, proclaiming itself the second highest in Europe. East of the house water pours from jets in the

Local lead-miners' courts provided stocks, like these at Chapel

Chatsworth's beautiful natural setting is complemented by fine gardens

Cascade House on the hillside, and tumbles over terraced steps before disappearing into the ground. Above that is thick woodland which climbs a steep cliff to the Hunting Tower, a gazebo built in Elizabethan times when Sir William and Lady Cavendish – Bess of Hardwick – were laying out the first Chatsworth House.

The present mansion displaced it between 1678 and 1707. Dutch architect, William Talman, was employed by the 4th Earl to alter Bess's house in the Classical manner, but the two styles proved to be incompatible. So did the Earl and Talman, who left. Later, the Earl, who became the 1st Duke in 1694, decided on a total rebuild to his own designs – with advice and help from Thomas Archer. The only major change since then has been the addition of the north, or Theatre, wing by Sir Jeffry Wyatville for the 6th 'Bachelor' Duke in 1820.

James Paine laid out the present road through the park in the 1760s, the previous one having run east and west across the grain of the country. He also built the two charming bridges, and the stables north of the house. Around the same time Capability Brown landscaped the park and altered the course of the river.

The estate village of Edensor (pronounced Ensor), which was formerly between the river and the road, was moved to its present site by the 6th Duke between 1838 and 1842. Sir Joseph Paxton – who was head gardener and almost managing director of Chatsworth, as well as an architect, writer and business tycoon – planned the village and designed some of the houses. The others are the work of J C Robertson, and no two are alike. Paxton also designed some of the houses in the estate village of Pilsley, to the west of the park, though a number of its buildings are older and date from the 18th century.

Chatsworth deserves a long, leisurely visit. It contains work by the finest craftsmen and artists, and its grounds are equally rewarding.

Chelmorton

Map Ref: 91SK1170

By a Bronze Age tumulus on Chelmorton Low (1,440ft) rises a stream that is delightfully if inexplicably called Illy Willy Water. It was this which dictated the shape of the village, which has a single street along which most of its farms are strung with their crofts laid out behind in the medieval style. Only six remain of the 20 or so that were once worked here. At the top of the street, just below the Low, is the medieval church of St John the Baptist. Church Inn stands immediately opposite and early 18th-century Townsend Farm is the full-stop at the end of the village.

The Peak's narrow fields are among the earliest of the district's enclosures

One of the most important things about Chelmorton is its pattern of 'fossil' arable strips within drystone walls enclosed by agreement from medieval times. Originally the complex was a single Open Field enclosed within an earth bank, part of which remains. Outside lay the common pasture. Beyond, stretching to the parish boundary, are neatly regular fields laid out by the Enclosure Commissioners after the 1809 Enclosure Award.

To quote from an official report, what the visitor sees here 'is an example of an historic landscape which is perhaps not seen to better effect anywhere else in Britain'. The Park Board is taking steps to ensure that it stays that way.

Chesterfield

Map Ref: 81SK3871

Formerly a coal-mining centre and still a busy industrial focus, Chesterfield is a lively red-brick town totally different in appearance and character from anywhere in the Peak. It is also a good base from which to explore the eastern half of the National Park, and the start of a dramatic drive across the moors on the A619 to Baslow. Half way along the road a stone wall separates green fields from brown moorland. No change could be more sudden.

Chesterfield has its own attractions. Best known and most obvious is the crooked spire of St Mary and All Saints Church, basically the result of incompatibility between lead and unseasoned timber – although there are more colourful explanations. The church itself testifies to the prosperity of the town, particularly its guilds, in the first half of the 14th century. Parts of the fabric are a century earlier, and the building's size and grandeur – plus the importance of Chesterfield as Derbyshire's second town – only narrowly failed to win it cathedral status when the Derby Diocese was created in 1927. Inside are many fine monuments, particularly those of the Foljambe family at the east end of the Lady Chapel.

Chesterfield's spire twisted because unseasoned timber was used in its construction

Local public opinion saved the spacious market place from development in the 1970s, and along with much more of the town centre it now forms part of a conservation area. Its most interesting building is probably the former Peacock Inn, which on the eve of demolition was found to be a medieval timber-framed structure. Probably the town house of a prominent local family, it has been restored as nearly as possible to its original form and is used as a heritage and information centre.

A leisurely inspection of Chesterfield above the modern shop

Engineer George Stephenson's quarry at Crich now contains a tram museum

fronts reveals a number of good old buildings of different periods, and some very presentable modern ones. Of particular note is the new County Library. Farther out in the northern suburb of Whittington, which has kept much of its original village core, is the much-restored, stone-built 16th-century Revolution House. Now a small museum, this was the inn where a number of aristocratic plotters – including the 4th Earl of Devonshire – planned the Great Rebellion of 1688 and resultant abdication of James II in favour of William and Mary.

South-east of that is Tapton House, a late Georgian building which is now a school but once was the home of the great railway engineer, George Stephenson. Here in retirement he carried out experiments in horticulture, and one trade paper announced his death in 1848 under the headline, 'Inventor of Straight Cucumber Dies'. He was buried in Holy Trinity Church, Newbold Road, where the stained glass in the east window is a memorial to him.

AA recommends:
Hotels: Chesterfield, Malkin St, 3-star, *tel.* (0246) 271141
Portland, West Bars, 2-star, *tel.* (0246) 234502
Campsite: Mill Farm, Barlow, Venture Site, *tel.* (0742) 890543 (on B6051)
Garage: Hawksley Service Station, Hawksley Ave, Newbold, *tel.* (0246) 271661

Crich

Map Ref: 81SK3554

George Stephenson owned both Crich Cliff Quarry and the gravity-incline railway that carried stone down a 1-in-7 slope from the cliff face to his battery of lime-kilns alongside the Cromford Canal, and to the Midland Railway in the

Derwent Valley. The last load was handled in 1957, and since 1959 the quarry floor has been occupied by the Crich Tramway Museum. Here trams that may once have clanged through the streets of Prague or Opporto carry visitors past Edwardian street advertisements, and out along a ridge which affords superb views.

Above the quarry, on Crich Cliff, is a light which shines out every night from the top of Crich Stand – a memorial tower 950ft above sea level which commemorates those soldiers of the Sherwood Foresters (the Nottinghamshire and Derbyshire Regiment) who fell in two wars. The tower is open daily, offering magnificent views extending from Lincoln Cathedral in the east to the Wrekin summit far away in the west.

Fourth on or near the site, the tower stands on an island of limestone surrounded by gritstone. The large, straggling hill village itself – once a market town, with a medieval market cross as evidence – has other surprises. Among the most picturesque is an 18th-century framework knitters' cottage of three storeys and a long upper window. Also interesting is a four-fold horse trough, probably for the pack-horse teams which crossed these hills carrying lead and stone.

The church of St Michael, partly Norman and with a Norman font, has a built-in stone lectern (rare outside Derbyshire), and some good monuments. One is to Sir William de Wakebridge (died 1369), who founded two chantries after losing his wife, father, two brothers and three sisters in the Black Death. Another recalls John Claye (died 1632), whose wife's father was 'unto that king of fame Henrie the Eight, chief cock-matcher and servant of his hawkes. . . .'

Neighbouring Fritchley was an important Quaker centre in the 19th and early 20th centuries, and still has a flourishing Quaker chapel. It also has clear traces of a pre-Stephenson railway (or tramway), built around 1780 to take stone from another Crich quarry to lime kilns on the canal at Bull Bridge.

Cromford

Map Ref: 93SK2956

Here in 1771 Richard Arkwright built the first successful water-powered cotton mill (see panel below), but that is by no means all there is to Cromford. For instance, the village is also the site of his two homes – pseudo-Gothic Willersley Castle, which was completed only just before his death in 1792; and Rock House, which looks down on his first mills and on the restored basin of the Cromford Canal. The former is now used as a Methodist guest house.

Cromford Canal Society runs horse-drawn boat trips on summer weekends to nearby Leawood Pump House, where a restored Watt-type beam-engine is periodically in steam. Just beyond the pump house is William Jessop's spectacular Wigwell Aqueduct, which carries the canal high over the river valley.

Between Leawood and Cromford the canal passes High Peak Junction, the terminus of the Cromford and High Peak Railway. Completed in 1831, it was the first line to cross the Peak from south east to north west. Stationary engines hauled wagons up the steeper gradients, but locomotives operated on the more level portions. After its last section, the Middleton Incline (see Wirksworth) closed in 1967, the track was adapted as the High Peak Trail – a 17½-mile route for walkers, cyclists and horse-riders.

Near the canal basin the Derwent is spanned by a three-arched 15th-century bridge, with the ruins of a contemporary bridge chapel alongside. The early 18th-century fishing temple close by is a replica of the Walton-Cotton one in Beresford Dale.

Water Power

Cromford, just off the A6 as it approaches the Matlocks, has a spacious, urban air about it that is unusual in such an apparent backwater. The broad market square is backed by the solid presence of the Greyhound Inn, and up The Hill towards Wirksworth, rows of neat, gritstone terraces give the impression of a carefully-planned township.

The answer lies just across the A6 down Mill Lane, where the gaunt, fortress-like buildings of Upper Mill give the final clue to Cromford's past importance. For it was here that a 'bag-cheeked, pot-bellied Lancashire man' known as Richard Arkwright came in 1771 to build the first water-powered cotton mill, and so transform textile manufacturing from a cottage to a factory industry.

It was the power of the River Derwent, which Daniel Defoe had called 'that fury of a river', and its tributaries which first brought the Preston-born barber and wig-maker to Cromford. Its very isolation, away from the prying eyes of competitors and close to a cheap, unorganised and plentiful supply of labour from the declining lead mines, must have been a major attraction.

Yet in the end, it was Cromford's isolation which was to prevent it becoming another Manchester. Poor communications and the distance from ports like Liverpool, where the raw cotton came in, eventually saw Cromford's decline – although Arkwright was to amass a personal fortune in 20 years which would allow him to boast he could liquidate the whole of the national debt.

Arkwright, the semi-literate genius who was the thirteenth child of a poor family, was to build three mills in the village – of which Masson Mill, built in 1784, is still used for textile manufacture. Arkwright's planned township of Cromford was not his only presence in the Peak District. Upstream on the River Wye he created Lumford Mill at Bakewell and the original Cressbrook Mill in Miller's Dale.

That 'furious river' and others like it had been used for centuries, of course, mainly for corn-grinding mills, but also for crushing mineral ores, pulping rags for paper, and even for grinding and polishing Ashford Black Marble.

One corn mill still grinds flour powered by the River Wye at Rowsley, where a dedicated band of enthusiasts operate Caudwell's Mill in much the same way as it has been for over a century. Remains of other corn mills still exist in Chatsworth Park (in ruins), at Over Haddon and Alport-by-Youlgreave. Bobbin mills at Ashford in the Water used the surrounding ash and sycamore woods as raw materials for another necessity in the textile trade.

Another fine old mill building, later to be used as a backdrop to the television series *Colditz* and now involved in the production of stainless steel products, is Calver Mill, built by John Gardom in 1804.

Edale Mill, built in 1795 by Nicholas Cresswell, has been restored by the Landmark Trust, while Bamford Mill (1780), now produces electric furnaces and laboratory equipment.

Owners like Arkwright prided themselves on the provision they made for their workforces, which consisted mainly of women and children. Not all millowners were as benevolent, however, and the 1828 *Memoirs* of Robert Blincoe, employed by Ellis Needham at Litton Mill on the Wye, were a catalogue of cruelty and degradation. Modern scholars now believe they were 'ghosted' pieces of propaganda in support of long-overdue changes in factory laws.

Arkwright's mills led the world in using water-powered machinery

Darley Dale

Map Ref: 93SK2762

A romantically-minded vicar and commercially-minded Midland Railway Company have both been credited with devising this 19th-century name for the seemingly endless ribbon of buildings alongside the A6 north of Matlock – a sort of elongated centre for the collection of older and smaller settlements established along a spring-line east of the Derwent.

The name, the railway and the setting attracted both picknickers and commuters. Many of the former were from Manchester, and most of the latter were railwaymen – with the notable exception of Sir Joseph Whitworth, inventor of the screw thread. He bought Stancliffe Hall, built cottages for his estate workers, laid out new roads to ease his own passage to the station and eventually left to the village an hotel, institute and a hospital named after him. All this had been intended to form the nucleus of a much larger model village.

For his construction Whitworth used stone from the nearby Stancliffe Quarry, source of building material for fine architecture that included the Thames Embankment, Hyde Park Corner and the Walker Art Gallery in Liverpool.

The medieval parish church of St Helen is a fine cruciform building standing in the hamlet of Churchtown, between the A6 and the river. In the churchyard are the ancient, battered remains of a once-huge yew tree, which is still 33ft in circumference 4ft from the ground.

Near by, 15th-century Darley Bridge carries the B5057 Winster road over the Derwent below isolated Oaker Hill (634ft), which is crowned by twin sycamores. North of the bridge are the remains of Mill Close Mine, the largest and most productive Derbyshire lead mine until flooding caused its abandonment in 1938.

AA recommends:
Garage: Two Dales Service Station, Warney Rd, *tel.* (0629) 733746

Dovedale

Map Ref: 95SK1452

Possibly the most beautiful of all the Derbyshire dales – and thanks to Walton and Cotton, clearly the best known – Dovedale often hosts as many as 4,000 visitors on a sunny Sunday afternoon. Most tend to stay near the stepping stones, however, leaving the remaining 2½ miles uncluttered.

In its 45-mile course from Axe Edge to the Trent, the Dove is essentially a walker's river almost inaccessible by car. This seclusion, along with its literary associations, the clarity of its tumbling water, its

Conical Thorpe Cloud broods mysteriously over the famous beauties of Dovedale, a place as notable for its varied wildlife as it is for its splendid scenery

steep wooded sides, its white rocks carved into fantastic shapes by weather and water – and above all, the way it unfolds its beauty gradually, ever enticing the visitor on to see what lies beyond the next gracious curve – contributes greatly to the charm of Dovedale. At its end is Viator's Bridge and a short stretch of road to Lode Mill, then another 5 miles of enchantment woven by the magical Wolfscote and Beresford Dales.

The main car park for Dovedale is below Bunster Hill, on the Staffordshire side of the river, which can be crossed either by bridge or the famous stepping stones. A smaller, newer car park is sited at Mill Dale, the only settlement anyone has managed to squeeze into the gorge. There is no long-term parking in Thorpe, the nearest village, except for residents at the hotel and guest houses. Accommodation began to spring up early in the 19th century, when a new enthusiasm for romantic scenery led to the area's 'discovery'.

Recently, more places to stay and bicycle-hire facilities have been provided, but so discreetly that Thorpe remains a charmingly unsophisticated limestone village.

Its little church has a west tower, belfry windows and a font which are all of early-Norman date. The early 14th-century nave has limestone rubble walls of various thicknesses, giving them the appearance of leaning outward, and the curious churchyard sundial is too tall to be read except from horseback. Beyond the church the village street degenerates into a track leading to 18th-century Coldwall Bridge, which has carried just a green lane since having been deserted by its turnpike road when it proved too steep for cars.

From the village a pleasant walk through Lin Dale leads down to the stepping stones below Thorpe Cloud ('clud' means 'a hill'), a much climbed cone rising to 942ft. Like most of Dovedale, it is owned by the National Trust.

AA recommends:
Hotels: ◇ Izaak Walton, Thorpe, 3-star, *tel.* (033529) 261 (1m W on llam rd)
◇ Peveril of the Peak, Thorpe, 3-star, *tel.* (033529) 333
Self Catering: ◇ Coldwall & Green Cottages, Digmire Lane, Thorpe, *tel.* (033529) 447
Guesthouse: ◇ Hillcrest House, Thorpe, *tel.* (033529) 436

Edale

Map Ref: 87SK1285

Civilisation ceases at Edale. 'No turning space for cars beyond this point', says the sign at the top of the village. Beyond it the road stops and the skyline is jagged with the highest, wildest hills of the mysterious Dark Peak.

Here, at the Nag's Head, is where the Pennine Way starts its 250-mile northward march to the Scottish border at Kirk Yetholm. Almost at once the route divides, one path heading north up Grindsbrook, and the other west up Jacob's Ladder to Edale Cross. They meet again by Kinder Downfall – the Peak's highest waterfall – on the 2,088ft boggy peat plateau of Kinder Scout. This is the highest point in the National Park.

Neither route, nor any other walk on the tops north of Edale, should be attempted without proper equipment and some indications of weather conditions. Sudden squalls, mists and dramatic temperature changes are features of this wild and dangerous country, where the going can be extremely tough.

Up-to-date weather and other information is always available from the National Park Information Centre at Fieldhead, between Edale church and the railway station. Maps and guides can be bought there too, and a permanent exhibition deals with the history of the area – majoring on Edale village in particular.

Edale began as a loose confederation of scattered settlements called booths, originally the 'bothies' or huts which give temporary shelter to shepherds and herdsmen tending their beasts on the summer pastures. Upper, Barber, Grindsbrook, Oller and Nether Booths became one parish, carved out of Castleton in 1863. By then Nether Booth had a cotton mill, which now serves as holiday accommodation and is owned by the Landmark Trust.

Otherwise, Edale has always been – and remains – a dairy farming and stock-rearing area, to which tourism has been added since the arrival of the Sheffield-Manchester branch line in 1894. Those early visitors could only gaze at moors reserved for grouse and gamekeepers. That the Church Hotel became the Railway Hotel and is now the Ramblers' Hotel tells its own concise tale of Edale's changing priorities.

A former Nag's Head landlord – the late Mr Fred Heardman – and his customers began an unofficial mountain-rescue service which has grown into the Peak District Mountain Rescue Organisation. The inn was built in 1577, probably to serve drivers of packhorse teams carrying Cheshire salt across the Peak. A packhorse bridge still spans tumbling Grinds Brook just below the late 16th-century, mullioned-windowed Waterside Cottage.

Besides its hotels, Edale has adventure and walking centres, camping and caravan sites, a large Youth Hostel, bed-and-breakfast accommodation and a residential youth centre at Champion House – run jointly by Derby Diocese and the Derbyshire County Council.

The only road to the village follows the course of the River Noe from Hope, then winds over Mam Nick. From that section there are magnificent views over the green Vale of Edale.

AA recommends:
Campsite: Coopers Caravan Site, Newfold Farm, 2-pennants *tel.* (0433) 70372
Self Catering: ◇ Flat 3, Edale Mill, *tel.* (062882) 5925

The Peak's first mountain-rescue service was formed in the Nag's Head, Edale

Elton

Map Ref: 95SK2261

In Elton the main street follows a long, flat ledge where limestone and gritstone meet at over 900ft above sea level. On one side are lime-loving flowers and a few ash trees, and on the other thrives gritstone vegetation with a scattering of oaks. The houses reflect this dichotomy, some being of limestone, more of gritstone and the majority a mixture of each. This is seen to advantage in the many 17th- and 18th-century houses that survive – like the Old

Hall, now a Youth Hotel, which is dated 1688. It has a more recent extension of 1715.

Although the surrounding countryside looks hard, water lies close to the surface and the moorland is good for rearing both sheep and cattle. It was also rich in lead, and until recently the villagers – as elsewhere in the uplands – practised the dual economy of mining and farming.

A mile north on Harthill Moor are curious outcrops of gritstone – like Robin Hood's Stride, which has terminal monoliths that are 22yds apart. Both it and Cratcliff

Tor provide good rock-climbing training. In a shallow cave at the Tor foot, a medieval hermit carved out a crucifix, a stone steat and a niche for a candle.

The River Bradford rises one mile north-west of Elton at Dale End, below Gratton Moor. This area, like Harthill Moor, is littered with prehistoric tumuli.

Eyam

Map Ref: 88SK2176

Infamous as a 17th-century plague village (see panel below). Eyam (pronounced 'Eem') is a large, almost self-contained and very typical mineral mining and quarrying settlement with a fascinating history well documented by informative wall plaques and an excellent exhibition in the church.

In the churchyard are the Peak's best-preserved Saxon cross, an unusual sundial of 1775 and some interesting headstones – including a very English one to Derbyshire cricketer Harry Bagshaw. The church building itself has been much restored, but its Saxon and Norman fonts, Jacobean woodwork and medieval wall paintings should be seen. Indeed, the whole village deserves a careful study for its fascinating variety of local vernacular building styles.

The Plague Village

The Riley Graves are a sad reminder of the Eyam villagers' brave sacrifice

Eyam is a busy, hard-working village nestling at the foot of Sir William Hill, above the limestone cliffs of Middleton Dale. The name, pronounced 'Eem', is thought to come from the Old English word meaning 'an island'. In the fateful years from 1665 to 1666, Eyam certainly *did* become an island, in what has been described as one of the most epic stories in the annals of rural life. The self-imposed quarantine of the tiny village when the dread plague virus arrived – so the infection would not spread farther – has made Eyam a place of pilgrimage ever since.

Three centuries later there are still many poignant reminders in the village of those terrible days, when 259 people from 76 families died. Many of the houses where the killer disease struck still stand, and neatly-painted signs give the names of the victims. Perhaps the most touching relic of those black days is to be

found in a field about half a mile east of the village. There, in a lonely little walled enclosure known as the Riley Graves, are the simple memorials to a father, his three sons and three daughters – all of whom died within eight days of each other in August 1666. It must be presumed that they were all buried by the distraught mother. They were all members of the Hancock family, but the tragedy had struck even harder at the neighbouring farm of the Talbots during the previous month, when a whole family of seven was wiped out.

It is thought the virus arrived in Eyam in a box of cloth brought up from plague-hit London by a journeyman tailor known as George Viccars, who lodged with the Widow Cooper in the cottages just west of the church. A few days later on 7 September 1665 the first grim entry was made in the deaths regis-

ter by the young rector William Mompesson, as Viccars was buried. A fortnight later one of Widow Cooper's sons, Edward, died of the same symptoms, and the following day a neighbour, Peter Halksworth, also succumbed.

Rumours of the deadly nature of the disease must have spread through the population like wildfire, but it was the young rector – aided by his non-Conformist predecessor Thomas Stanley – who united the village in the courageous decision not to flee, but to try to contain the outbreak within the community.

The decision was communicated to the Earl of Devonshire, the lord of the manor, who arranged for provisions, clothing and medical supplies to be left for collection at certain points around the village boundary such as Mompesson's Well. Here coins were left in the water, disinfected in vinegar, as payment. Mompesson, having sent his own children away shortly after the outbreak, had the heartrending task of burying his wife Katherine on 25 August 1666. Her table tomb is in the churchyard, near the ancient Saxon cross.

This touching and tragic story of the plague is remembered on the last Sunday of August every year, with a Commemoration Service held in the open air at Cucklet Church, a natural limestone cavern where Mompesson had held his services during the 'visitation' 300 years ago.

Villages like Foolow depended on their meres (ponds) as reliable sources of water

Foolow and the Hucklows

Map Ref: 88SK1976

Foolow sits attractively round a large green – a rare Peakland feature – with a village cross, bull-ring and mere at the centre, and a well at the edge. Its lead mines have closed, though two mine hillocks are distantly visible. So have its farms, except on the outskirts. Commuters now occupy the farmhouses and their outbuildings, tastefully converted into 'desirable residences of character' – among them a pigsty and neighbouring cow-stall. The 18th-century Spread Eagle Inn is a private house too, though its tethering-rings for horses (the Georgian equivalent of a car-park), hint at its past. The Bull's Head is the sole surviving pub of five that once stood here.

The Barrell Inn at Bretton, which has overlooked Foolow from 1,200ft on Eyam Edge since at least 1637, has recently been skilfully restored.

Camphill, 2 miles east of Bretton, on Hucklow Edge, is the headquarters of the Lancashire and Derbyshire Gliding Club. Venue of the 1954 World Gliding Championships, it is a place where visitors can watch gliding every weekend in the year, or join a five-day holiday course.

Below the Edge is Great Hucklow, 'great' only in comparison with Little Hucklow (2 miles north-west), and the closer Grindlow, having roughly half the combined population of about 260. Inspired by Laurence du Garde Peach, of *Punch* magazine, who lived near by, it supported live theatre in an old lead-smelting works from 1927 to 1971. Audiences once travelled miles to the shows.

AA recommends:
Campsite: Brosterfield Farm, Venture Site, *tel.* (0433) 30958 (½m S on unclass rd & ¼m N of A623)
Self Catering: ◇ South View Cottage, Great Hucklow, *tel.* (0298) 871440

Glossop was developed as a 19th-century milltown by the 11th Duke of Norfolk

Glossop

Map Ref: 82SK0394

A 10-minute car journey from Norfolk Square in Glossop is all that separates the town from the point between Featherbed Moss and Shelf Moor (1,600ft) where the Pennine Way crosses the A57 Snake Road. In winter this is closed nearly as often as it is open, but on good days it is an exhilarating drive. Over the central watershed the road follows the line of the medieval Doctor's Gate – named after a Dr Talbot, who rediscovered it – and drops down through Woodlands Valley, past the Snake Inn and accompanies the River Ashop until it widens into Ladybower Reservoir. It then crosses the Ashopton Viaduct and continues to the city of Sheffield.

Glossop is an oddly civilised departure point for this drive over the wilderness, being an early 19th-century planned town, well laid out with suitable dignified squares and public buildings for the 11th Duke of Norfolk at a point where three turnpike roads crossed the Glossop Brook. At that time the waterway had already been harnessed to provide driving power for machinery in three new cotton mills.

As an outlier of the then booming Lancashire cotton industry, the new 'Howardstown' outgrew the original village of Glossop and took its name when the municipal borough was formed in 1876. Old Glossop remains as an unspoilt, suburban enclave containing a number of 17th-century houses.

Dinting Railway Centre, one mile west of Glossop, is open daily (except Christmas Day). Near by is the splendid Dinting Viaduct, and a further mile north-west is the 19-acre fort site of Roman *Melandra*, on the edge of the vast, modern, Gamesley housing estate.

AA recommends:
Hotels: Colliers Hotel & Restaurant, 14/14A High St East, *tel.* (04574) 63409 Wind in the Willows, Derbyshire Level, 2 star *tel.* (04574) 68001 (due to change to (0457) 868001 (off A57)

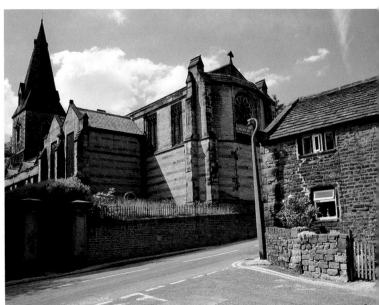

Goyt Valley

Map Ref: 90SK0172

The lovely upper reaches of the River Goyt (see Axe Edge) are best approached from Buxton and Long Hill (A5002) down a 1-in-7 gradient by Bunsall Incline – once the steepest on the Cromford and High Peak Railway. Motorists should tackle the few narrow lanes in the area with care, and never on Sundays or bank holidays – except to the car parks. The Goyt may have been 'little known to tourists', as a guide book said 80 years ago, but not now.

The valley has changed too, since Stockport Corporation dammed the Goyt to form two reservoirs – Fernilee in 1938 and Errwood in 1967. However, it is still beautiful in a slightly different way. In June the rhododendrons light up the otherwise sombre ruins of Errwood Hall, built by the Grimshawe family in 1830 but abandoned when the estate was depopulated for the reservoir. The whole valley is noted for its rich vegetation.

AA recommends:
Campsite: ◇ Ringstones Caravan Park, Yeardsley Ln, Furness Vale, *tel.* (06633) 2152

Water and woodland in a striking natural combination typical of the Goyt Valley

Grindleford and the Padleys

Map Ref: 89SK2478

Grindleford Bridge spans the Derwent in a lovely setting between Eyam Moor and Froggatt Edge, at the apex of a triangle of roads. From there a minor route climbs west to curve round the lower slopes of Sir William Hill into Eyam, with a branch to Hucklow Edge. The B6001 runs north to Hathersage, and the B6521 north east across the river and up through trees to Fox House Inn – named after a man called Fox.

From Grindleford Station – actually in Upper Padley – along the B6521 is a track that leads beside the railway to the sparse ruins of Padley Manor House. Once the home of two devout Roman Catholic families, in 1588 the house witnessed the arrest of priests Nicholas Garlick and Robert Ludlam. Twelve days after being taken to Derby they, and another unfortunate, were hanged, drawn and quartered. Owner of the house Thomas Fitzherbert died in the Tower of London in 1591, and his

Medieval Haddon Hall's impressive military air is purely decorative, although in every way authentic

brother John in Fleet Prison in 1598. The house was sold in 1657.

In 1933 the Roman Catholic Nottingham Diocese bought the original hall range and converted what had become a cowshed into a delightful chapel, to which a pilgrimage is made each July.

AA recommends:
Hotel: Maynard Arms, Main Rd, 3-star, *tel.* (0433) 30321

Haddon Hall

Map Ref: 93SK2366

On rising ground above the Wye and its meadows is the 'ideal' medieval manor house, a beautiful building with a perfection to which every century from the 12th to the 17th has contributed. After 1640 it lay fallow because its owners, the Manners family – Earls and then Dukes of Rutland – made Belvoir Castle in Leicestershire their main residence. Then, this century, the father of the present Duke devoted most of his life to its scrupulously accurate restoration. It thus escaped any changes which may otherwise have resulted from the whims of fashion.

That it dodged military involvement also assisted its preservation – the turrets and battlements were just for show.

The earliest work is seen in the chapel, along with examples from all the other building periods. Sir John Manners added the impressive long gallery to the banquetting hall, kitchen, dining room, great chamber and 12ft perimter wall built by earlier residents, the Vernon family, and when it was finished in 1597 the building

Grindleford Bridge spans the Derwent at a junction of moorland roads

history of the house came to a complete and fitting end.

As to the story of the elopement of Dorothy Vernon and John Manners, neither the Dorothy Vernon Steps nor the bridge on which she allegedly joined her lover were there in her time. That, however, does not necessarily invalidate the tale, which – true or false – suits the environment.

Hartington

Map Ref: 94SK1260

This gracious limestone village still has the atmosphere of the market town it became in 1204, featuring a spacious market place that may once have been a green, a battlemented cruciform church with a dignified Perpendicular tower, a reasonably comprehensive range of shops and services, and a population of around 400. The actual parish is so vast that it was divided into four quarters – Upper, Nether, Middle and Town – the names of which still appear on maps.

Standing on the River Dove where its valley widens north of Beresford Dale, Hartington is a good centre from which to explore the Dove and Manifold valleys, and the central limestone uplands to the east. It offers good food it its several inns, good angling, pleasant walking and the opportunity for a peaceful half hour admiring the ducks on the village mere. The buildings are worthy of study too, being typical of the Peak and built of limestone – dressed or just plain rubble – with the more workable gritstone used for mullions, quoins and other architectural features.

Hartington Hall, a typical 17th-century Peakland manor house was enlarged in the 19th century and now serves as a Youth Hostel. On rising ground east of the village, it numbers Bonnie Prince Charlie among its early guests. West of the village square Stilton is produced in the only cheese factory left in Derbyshire, where once there were a great many more.

The cheese, in a variety of plain, veined and flavoured forms, can be bought from a dairy shop near the village mere.

Above the river, 3 miles north at Pilsbury, are strange earthworks which may be the remains of a Norman motte-and-bailey castle built on the site of an Iron Age fort.

AA recommends:
Hotel: Charles Cotton, 1-star, *tel.* (029884) 229
Campsite: ◇ Barracks Farm Caravan Site, Beresford Dale, 1-pennant, *tel.* (029884) 261

The Real Cost of Water

The deep gritstone dales and high rainfall of the Peak were a tempting prospect to the water engineers of the late 19th century, seeking to slake the ever-growing thirsts of the industrial cities on the surrounding lowlands.

Today, there are more than 50 reservoirs in the National Park, providing another entirely man-made element in the Peak District landscape. Despite their unnatural origins, they are often very popular with visitors and an enlightened attitude by the water authorities has seen many of them serve a dual purpose by providing numerous recreational opportunities.

The most famous series of reservoirs in the Peak are those which have flooded the Upper Derwent Valley in the east of the National Park. The triple chain of Howden, Derwent and Ladybower reservoirs, usually known as 'the Dams', represent the largest area of water space in the area and have been dubbed the Peak's Lake District.

It was in 1899 that the Derwent Valley Water Board was set up with the original purpose of constructing six reservoirs (later to be reduced to three) in the Derwent and Ashop valleys to serve the cities of Derby, Nottingham, Leicester and Sheffield with drinking water. The first two to be constructed were the Howden, highest up the valley in the shadow of Bleaklow, between 1901 and 1912, and the Derwent, which was built between 1902 and 1916.

To accomplish this massive project of civil engineering, a large workforce of navvies (so called because they first worked on the canal 'navigations') was needed. The DVWB resolved at an early stage 'to approve the erection of a village on a site near Birchinlee' which would house these nomadic workmen and their families over the 15 years of the contract.

The result was the extraordinary community of Birchinlee, popularly known as 'Tin Town' or 'Tin City' because of the green-painted, corrugated iron walls of the workmen's huts. Up to 1,000 people lived here in nearly 100 buildings, including shops, a recreation hall, a school, a hospital, a 'canteen' (as the pub was known) and a police station.

Only a few scattered hill farms went under the waters of the Howden and Derwent Reservoirs, and today nearly every trace of Tin Town is gone. However, when the larger Ladybower Reservoir was constructed between 1935 and 1943, the villages of Derwent and Ashopton had to be sacrificed under the rising waters. The villagers were rehoused in purpose-built accommodation at Yorkshire Bridge, just below the massive earthwork embankment of the dam, but many memories of their communities remain.

Among the buildings lost were the stately pile of Derwent Hall – dating from 1672 and a home of the Dukes of Norfolk, later to become one of the first Youth Hostels in the Peak – and the parish church of St John and St James, Derwent.

Another stately mansion which was demolished by the water engineers for reasons of water purity was Errwood Hall, the Victorian home of the Grimshawe family in the Goyt Valley.

Today, these water-filled valleys – often surrounded by dense coniferous forests – are a magnetic attraction to visitors. Traffic-management schemes, picnic areas and car parks have been provided to increase their enjoyment of these man-made landscapes.

A Derwent Valley landscape of reservoir-side plantations

Sherwood outlaw Little John is said to lie in this grave at Hathersage

Hathersage

Map Ref: 89SK2381

The A625 swoops down into Hathersage from the aptly-named Surprise View, where the land falls away suddenly to reveal an astonishing panorama of the hills around Kinder, across the valleys of the Noe and Derwent – whose waters meet on the village fringe.

Hathersage itself is large and prosperous, with hotels and shops lining a main road which drops to cross the Derwent and then enters the Hope Valley by the junction with the B6001. Here on Christmas Eve worshippers of all denominations sing carols round a nativity group.

Less than 12 miles from Sheffield and linked to it by the Hope Valley line from Manchester since 1894, it is a lively place with more than 60 organisations. Included is a thriving historical society which produces a useful village trail. This informs the visitor that for most of the 19th century Hathersage was a centre of the needle, pin and wire-drawing industry, with the tall chimneys of five mills 'belching out thick black smoke'. The industry, the smoke and the back-to-back houses vanished around the turn of the century, but four mills remain. One has been converted into luxury flats, and they all fulfil new uses.

The village's main tourist attraction – apart from the open-air swimming pool – is the grave of Little John in the churchyard between yew trees 10ft apart. A 30in thigh-bone exhumed there in 1784 was subsequently stolen. The church, much restored by Butterfield in 1852, contains Eyre monuments which may have given Charlotte Brontë the surname for

her heroine in *Jane Eyre*. The Eyres reputedly held seven manor houses in Hathersage, of which North Leas was bought by the Peak Park Board in 1971. This Elizabethan tower house is now the nucleus of a farm, and parts of its 1,200-acre estate are open to the public.

The crags and tumbled rocks of Kinder Downfall, on the edge of Kinder Scout

Hayfield

Map Ref: 87SK0387

Where the boisterous little River Sett bustles down from the Kinder Massif on to relatively level ground, the tall gritstone buildings of Hayfield snuggle compactly along its narrow valley. The A624 road tumbles down from the 1,000ft contour line at Chinley Head to cut through the village on a new bypass, and then climbs sharply to reach 1,000ft again at attractive Hollingworth Head.

Some 1½ miles beyond Little Hayfield – dominated by Clough Mill in the west and Park Hall, whose nearest eastward neighbour is nearly 20 miles away on the other side of Kinder Scout – is a left turn on to the Charlesworth road, just short of the Grouse Inn. This leads along Monks Road – named after the monks of Basingwerk Abbey in Flint, who owned land hereabouts from the 12th to the 16th century – to Coombes Edge and a remarkable view of two Englands. All around is some of the wildest, emptiest land in the country, while below is the vast sprawl of matchbox buildings that is Greater Manchester. The scene could have been tailor-made for artist, L S Lowry, who lived on the edge of that uninspiring area at

Mottram-in-Longdendale.

Hayfield has a foot in both Englands, with an economy based on wool, water and walking. First came the sheep, whose wool was woven on frames in tall attics – then in even taller mills powered by the River Sett. Wool gave way to cotton, which was itself displaced by calico printing, and paper making in the 1860s. Now there is just one paper mill, but paint is manufactured in Clough Mill at Little Hayfield, sheep are still reared, and Hayfield remains the last refreshment stop for walkers tackling Edale Moor and Kinder Scout from the west – just as it was when the Pack Horse Inn was built in 1577 to cater for 'jaggers' (teamsmen) and their trains of 20 or 30 pack animals.

An incongruously urban subway funnels pedestrians under the bypass to Hayfield Station, now the start of the 2½-mile Sett Valley Trail for horse riders and walkers. The going along this old track is good and level, with no hard climbs.

Holmfirth

Map Ref: 83SE1408

Having narrowly missed becoming Britain's 'Hollywood', Holmfirth has achieved fame as the centre of *Last of the Summer Wine* country, where visitors who flock to the TV home of Foggy, Cleggy and Compo can follow in their footsteps by horse and trap provided by Nora Batty's Tours.

The village has been involved with the entertainment industry much longer than that, however, and was making pictures in 1870 when James Bamforth began producing magic lantern slides by photographing live models against his own hand-painted backcloths. He turned the slides into picture postcards as a successful sideline, and later in around 1908 progressed to movies. By then he was bringing professional players to Holmfirth by special trains to make films in the Holme Valley, but war ended production for good and Hollywood became dominant. The resourceful Bamforth concentrated then on comic postcards, inventing the seaside landlady and the stout female in a bathing costume whose grand daughters adorn postcards produced today by the family's modern generation.

The River Holme is a mere 8 miles long from its source at the foot of Holme Moss, below the 725ft mast of the BBC transmitter, to the River Colne at Huddersfield. It looks placid as it flows through the heart of Holmfirth, but three times in two centuries it has caused devastating floods with loss of life, 81 being drowned in the terrible disaster of 1852 when the nearby Bilberry Dam burst.

Holy Trinity Church was rebuilt after the 1777 flood as a most attractive Georgian 'preaching box',

with galleries on three sides and painted now in blue and white after the style of the better-known Shobbden Church in Herefordshire.

If the Sunday before Whitsun is wet, the 'Holmfirth Sing' is held in the church; if fine in Victoria Park. This community singing of hymns and *Messiah* selections, an annual event since 1882, grew from the Holmfirth Festival founded 1726.

Another annual event, the Harden Moss Sheepdog Trials, is held on two days in June on the moors off the A635 road.

AA recommends:
Guesthouse: White Horse, Scholes Rd, Jackson Bridge (inn), *tel.* (0484) 683940
Garage: G W Castle, Huddersfield Rd, *tel.* (0484) 683676

Hope

Map Ref: 88SK1783

Historically, this village is first mentioned in 926, when King Athelstan won a battle near by. By 1068 its parish embraced two-thirds of the Royal Forest of the High Peak, including Buxton, Tideswell

Beautifully dressed well at Hope

and Chapel-en-le-Frith, and a century ago it was still one of the largest in the country.

Of the original church mentioned in the *Domesday* survey, only the Norman font – recovered from the vicarage garden – remains. The present building, with its conspicuous, stumpy broach tower, dates mainly from 1200-1400 and was reroofed in stainless steel during the 1970s. The fine pulpit of 1652 bears the name of Thomas Bocking – vicar, schoolmaster and Royalist – whose chair in the north aisle bears a Latin inscription translatable as 'You cannot make a scholar out of a block of wood'. His 1599 'Breeches' Bible is exhibited near by. Two foliated 13th-century cross slabs with incised foresters' arms are memorials to Royal Forest officials.

The nearby Woodruffe Arms commemorates a local family who may once have held the office of wood reeve, and the 'Old Hall Hotel' was built in the early 17th century as a manor house for the Balguy family. They also built houses at Derwent and Aston, a centreless hamlet strung out along narrow lanes on a hillside to the east, and in 1715 obtained a charter for a market which is still held weekly. Nearly opposite the Old Hall is Daggers House (with cross-daggers engraved above the door), which was built in the 18th century as the Cross Daggers Inn. Along the Pin Dale road are the remains of a pinfold, where straying beasts were at one time impounded.

Although it has at least a dozen establishments offering bed and breakfast, Hope is perhaps less geared to tourism than neighbouring Castleton and Edale. However, it is undisputedly the educational centre for the valley, with its fine Hope Valley College having been opened in 1958.

AA recommends:
Restaurants: ◇ Poachers Arms, Castleton Rd, 3-forks, *tel.* (0433) 20380
Campsite: Laneside Caravan Park, Laneside Farm, 2-pennants, *tel.* (0433) 20214
Self Catering: ◇ Granary, Lime Loft & Stable Cottages, *tel.* (0433) 20214

TV fame came to Holmfirth with 'Last of the Summer Wine', featuring Nora Batty's House and Compo's wellies – seen here as a charity money box

Ilam and the Manifold Valley

Map Ref: 94SK1350

After rising close together on Axe Edge and following almost parallel courses, the Dove and Manifold merge near Ilam, a handsome estate village in romantic surroundings. Shipping magnate Jesse Watts Russell employed John Shaw to rebuild Ilam Hall in a battlemented Gothic style, and rebuild the whole village in the cottage *ornee* fashion. The tile-hanging and barge-boarded gables are unusual in the Peak – as too is the 30ft imitation Eleanor cross which he raised in memory of his first wife. In 1855, Gilbert Scott over-restored the ancient, saddleback-towered church, which was already dominated by Chantrey's overlarge monument to Russell's father-in-law, David Watts. Fortunately, he left undisturbed the shrine of St Bertelin (or Bertram), a late-Saxon saint.

When demolition of the hall began in 1934, Sir Robert McDougall bought what was left – along with parts of both the Dove and Manifold Valleys – and gave them to the National Trust. The hall is leased to the Youth Hostel Association. William Congreve wrote his bawdy play *The Old Bachelor*, and Dr Johnson received his inspiration for *Rasselas*, in the hall grounds.

The Manifold has many of the Dove's attributes, and its valley is only marginally less beautiful and usually decidedly less crowded – even though it has a good footpath along the track of the old Leek and Manifold Light Railway (1904-34).

The only part of the valley below Hulme End accessible to motorists is the short section between the former Redhurst Halt and Butterton Stations, it being too narrow for settlements. However, below Beeston Tor is a deserted village site

Thor's Cave, once home to prehistoric man, yawns hugely from its lofty crag above the Manifold Valley woodlands

and possible Romano-British settlement near the ruins of Throwley Hall. A scheme has been launched to conserve this area as a tourist attraction.

The Manifold villages are sited high above the gorge, and the entrance to Butterton is through an unusually long ford. Both Butterton and Grindon have architecturally uninspiring churches with prominent spires. The one at Grindon, on the edge of a common, contains a memorial to six RAF men who died when their aircraft crashed while 'bringing relief to the stricken villages during the great blizzard of 1947'. Two press photographers died with them, shortly after parachuting food supplies to the people of Wetton, Onecote, Butterton and Grindon.

In Wetton church is the grave of Samuel Carrington – village schoolmaster who, with Thomas Bateman of Middleton-by-Youlgreave, excavated a sizable Romano British settlement at Borough Fields and at Long Low. They discovered two round Late Neolithic cairns uniquely linked by a contemporary stone bank, and half a mile south west of the village at Thor's Cave found evidence of occupation through the Iron Age and Romano British times. The cave impressively overlooks the east bank of the Manifold.

Like the Manifold, the Hamps vanishes through its limestone bed on its course through charming, empty country. The nearest village, Waterfall, lies two miles west and is as pretty as its name, as is the tiny satellite of Back o' th' Brook.

AA recommends:
Campsite: Enden Cottage, Hulme End, Venture Site, *tel.* (029884) 617
Guesthouse: Beechenhill, Ilam (farmhouse), *tel.* (033527) 274

Leek

Map Ref: 80SJ9856

Cobbles, mills and sombre stone buildings give 'The Capital of the Moorlands' the forbidding appearance of a Lancashire cotton town that has somehow slipped into Staffordshire. However, there is more to this hillside town than that, including a charming little cobbled market place. The interesting church displays a variety of styles, with much stained glass by Morris & Co, and has two late-Saxon crosses in its churchyard. Leek's School of Needlework was founded by Elizabeth Wardle – later Lady Wardle – around 1870, and there is a James Brindley water mill which opens at weekends and on bank holidays.

A museum, library and art school are housed in 17th-century mansion of Greystones.

Leek's mills produced mainly silk goods and some cotton, hence the Leek Embroidery Society and its Bayeux Tapestry replica now housed in Reading Museum. The mills are used for dyeing, finishing and food processing purposes.

The wild and lovely moorland hinterland receives fewer visitors than it deserves. Only 2 miles south is the North Staffordshire Steam Railway Centre at Cheddleton Station, which runs a small museum and special steam weekends. Close by on the other side of the Churnet, where the re-opened Caldon Canal reaches the valley, are the restored buildings of the Cheddleton Flint Mill. From around 1800 flint was ground here for use in china manufacture. Nowadays the mill is open to visitors at weekends.

South from Cheddleton, the Churnet Valley is so steep-sided and

thickly wooded as to be inaccessible in places, even to walkers. Remains of industry are almost buried under vegetation, as at Consall Ironworks, but horse-drawn narrow boats from Froghall Wharf on Thursdays, Sundays and some Saturdays offer an enjoyable means of exploration.

In 1975 the Park Board bought the 975-acre Roaches Estate, north-east of Leek, to ensure its 'maximum public benefit in perpetuity'. Wonderful walking is available along the 2-mile serrated edge of this astonishing gritstone outcrop, with rock climbing too and superb views from 1,600ft of similar height ranges in all directions. Conical Hen Cloud rises half a mile to the south east.

AA recommends:
Hotel: Jester at Leek, 81 Mill St, 2-star, *tel.* (0538) 383997
Self Catering: ◇ Lowe Hill Cottages, Nos. 1 & 2, *tel.* (0538) 383035
Guesthouse: Peak Weavers Hotel, King St, *tel.* (0538) 383729
Holly Dale, Bradnop (farmhouse), *tel.* (0538) 383022

Typical Peakland house of the 18th century, one of many seen in Litton

Litton and Cressbrook

Map Ref: 88SK1675

Litton, clean-lined and compact among stone walls after the Chelmorton fashion, stands at almost 1,000ft on limestone uplands above the Wye. Its main street which has a triangular green at its western end and a wide strip of green down both sides, is a good place to study the vernacular architecture of the Peak. Many of the houses have date-stones – the earliest being 1639 – but the average is about a century later, towards the end of the period that Professor W G Hoskins called 'The Great Rebuilding'. It was a boom time in the local lead industry, too, which may explain the comparative lavishness of Clergy House (1723) and Hammerton House (1768). The combined church, school and library was given by Canon Samuel Andrews – vicar of Tideswell (then including Litton) – in 1865, and a

The Delightful Dales

John Ruskin, the 19th-century Romantic and early conservationist, was quite definite in his views of the respective merits of dale and moorland scenery in the Peak. 'The whole gift of the country is in its glens,' he claimed. 'The wide acreage of field or moor above is wholly without interest; it is only in the clefts of it, and the dingles, that the traveller finds his joy.'

River without water. Between Ilam and Wetton the Manifold flows underground

Most modern visitors would probably not be quite so dismissive of the rolling limestone plateau of the White Peak, with its fascinating relics from prehistory and its charming villages – but it is still the dales which dissect the plateau with their precipitous crags, verdant woodlands and nature reserves which provide the real scenic gems of the White Peak.

Geologists believe the dales were formed in the Carboniferous limestone at the end of the last Ice Age, when tremendous volumes of freezing melt water flowed out from the shrinking glaciers and snowfields, cutting through the rock like a knife through butter. Limestone, formed from the fossilised skeletons of sea-creatures some 330 million years ago, is a heavily-jointed rock that can be dissolved by rainwater.

This means that many of the White Peak dales are now dry, or only occasionally have a river flowing through them, as the water dives underground through swallet, swallow, or 'shakeholes'. Examples of this are the dramatic dry gorges of The Winnats and Cave Dale, near Castleton, and the disappearing rivers of the Manifold, Hamps, Bradford and Lathkill farther south.

What happens to the water when it disappears underground? The answer is it creates yet another, usually-unseen landscape of caves and caverns, which honeycomb the White Peak.

The 'hollow country' where the limestone and the gritstone, the White and Dark Peaks, meet around Castleton is where modern visitors can be introduced to the Peak's 'underground'. Well-lit show caves like Treak Cliff, Blue John, Speedwell and Bagshawe, at neighbouring Bradwell, attract thousands of visitors every year. The yawning void of Peak Cavern, beneath the ruins of Peveril Castle, is the largest cave entrance in Britain, and formerly housed a whole community of rope-makers. The soot from the chimneys of this subterranean village can still be seen in the cavern roof.

Thor's Cave, above the Manifold Valley near Wetton, is one of many Peakland caves which have revealed evidence of occupation by prehistoric man.

modern church was built in 1929. Litton retains close affinities with Tideswell, even to dressing its well on the same day – the Saturday which falls closest to St John the Baptist Day (24 June).

Cressbrook clings precariously to the lower slopes of the hillside above the Wye, its cottages terraced among ash woods. At the lowest level is a row that was formerly the apprentice house, where pauper apprentices from London and elsewhere lived during the short intervals between their long working days in Cressbrook Mill. They were well treated under William Newton, a local, self-made

business man and poet. Those at Litton Mill told a different story, as related by one, Robert Blincoe, who spent the worst years of his life there shortly after 1800.

Cressbrook Mill is a handsome building of 1815, partly used but in urgent need of restoration. The stretch of the Wye between the mills is known rather mysteriously as Water-Cum-Jolly (or Jolie). Cressbrook Dale is a pretty, thickly-wooded tributary valley running north from Monsal Dale.

AA recommends:
Guesthouse: Dale House (farmhouse), *tel.* (0298) 871309

Longnor

Map Ref: 91SK0965

In lonely moorland country on the River Manifold, Longnor still has something of the appearance and air of the market town it once was. At the upper end of a small, sloping and cobbled market place is a market house that was built in 1873, when Longnor was a prosperous farming community. A scale of market charges is posted on a board outside. The prosperity faded, however, as agricultural depression set in. The coaching age had already gone, the roads radiating from Longnor and its coaching inns were empty and the railway never arrived to fill the gap. Longnor's population declined from 561 in 1861 to 364 in 1981, with corresponding falls in most villages on this west side of the Peak.

Happily, the decline has been arrested, with the village having become a Conservation Area in 1977 and been the subject of much good restoration by the National Park authority. New workshops have been added in what the trade jargon calls an 'integrated rural development', a craftsman is at work in the market house, and a small industrial estate has been established on the outskirts.

Longnor is an excellent touring centre. North is a remarkable array of conical hills near the headwaters of the Dove, providing some of the Peak District's few genuine peaks. High Wheeldon (1,383ft) was given to the nation as a memorial to Derbyshire and Staffordshire men killed in World War II, then transferred to the National Trust. At its foot was a packhorse route that crossed the Dove at Crowdecote, whose Packhorse Inn preserves a packsaddle inside. The Quiet Woman Inn in the long, quarrying village of Earl Sterndale – tucked away between High Wheeldon and Parkhouse – shows a headless woman on its sign.

South-west of Longnor, the long, curving bulk of Morridge (Moor Edge) forms the natural western boundary of the National Park. The road along it, probably an ancient ridgeway, offers splendid views and leads at its northern end to the lonely Mermaid Inn – with its legend of a mermaid enticing strangers into the nearby Black Mere (or Mermaid Pool), and an apparently true story of a murder and another attempted killing.

AA recommends:
Restaurant: ◇ Ye Olde Cheshire Cheese, High St, 2-forks, *tel.* (029883) 218
Campsite: Dowall Hall, Glutton Bridge, Venture Site, *tel.* (029883) 272
Self Catering: ◇ Brund Mill Cottage, *tel.* (029884) 383
◇ 4 & 5 Chapel St, *tel.* (029884) 383
◇ No. 7 Chapel St (flat), *tel.* (029884) 383

Woodland is a pleasing contrast to the moors also in Longshaw Estate

Longshaw

Map Ref: 89SK2678

Over 1,500 acres of open moorland and woodland comprise the lovely Longshaw Estate, owned by the National Trust and designated a Country Park. At its heart is a

Horses must once have been a common sight in Longnor's old Market Place

former shooting lodge of the Dukes of Rutland.

Through the area – which extends from Fox House Inn to below Surprise View and includes Padley Wood – flows the Burbage Brook on its way south to the Derwent. Not far from its source north of the A625 road it runs below Carl Wark, a mysterious fortification on the edge of a plateau. Recent research suggests that it may date from considerably later than the various Iron Age forts in the Peak. On opposite sides of the brook at Lawrence Field and Sheffield Plantation are remnants of early village settlements.

South of the main road, relics of ancient natural woodland may have survived in parts of Padley Wood where the ground was too steep, rough and rocky for grazing sheep.

On the open moorland weathering has carved outcropping gritstone into strange and contorted shapes, such as Toad's Mouth Rock, near the road. The numerous millstones scattered around, especially near Millstone Edge, were presumably imperfect 'rejects'. The industry declined gradually after the introduction of roller mills in 1862. Sheep dog trials are held at Longshaw in early September.

Longstone

Map Ref: 92SK2071

Great Longstone, which is the larger of two, is an attractive, stone-built village stretching out from a small green and approached from the west along an avenue of elms. The Hall – a good, unfussy building of 1747 – is, surprisingly, of brick. This was presumably a piece of one-upmanship in an area abounding with building stone.

Little Longstone is strung out along the road a mile to the west and built wholly of stone, including the late 17th-century manor house and another of 1575.

A further half a mile to the west at the end of the road, the ground suddenly falls away to a stunning view of the River Wye running through Monsal Dale. The great stone Monsal Viaduct dominates the left foreground, beyond which rises Fin Cop with traces of an Iron Age fort at its summit.

Two miles east of Great Longstone is the little village of Hassop, dominated by the Roman Catholic Church of All Saints. It was built in 1816-18 for the Eyre family of Hassop Hall, an early 17th-century house enlarged around 1830 and now an hotel – with a lead-mine shaft in its cellar. Elegant Hassop Station, 2 miles south of the village, was built in 1863 by Edward Walters to serve the Duke of Devonshire rather than Hassop.

Classical south front of Lyme Park, and the interior of the orangery

It is now an agricultural implement depot on the Monsal Trail, a Park Board footpath which then continues over Monsal Viaduct.

Over all broods Longstone Edge (1,300ft), which affords good views and is the site of several tumuli. Fluorspar working has created some damage, though generally this has been well restored.

Lyme Park

Map Ref: 86SJ9682

When Sir Piers Legh married Margaret Danyers in 1388 he became the owner of Lyme Hanley in the Forest of Macclesfield, given in 1346 to her father Sir Thomas Danyers for services to Edward III in battle at Caen. Exactly 600 years later, Richard Legh, 3rd Lord Newton, gave Lyme Park to the National Trust – for whom it is administered by Stockport Borough Council.

The 7th of 11 Piers Leghs greatly enlarged an existing house in around 1570, and it is this Elizabethan work that forms the core of the present building. Little of it is visible from the outside, except on the north (entrance) front. Even there the substitution of later sash windows and the addition of end bays makes the 16th-century work less obvious.

Around this early house, to which a few piecemeal alterations had already been made, the Venetian architect Giacomo Leoni built a vast Palladian mansion with an impressive Ionic portico rising to three storeys on the south front facing the lake. Lewis Wyatt made further additions early in the 19th century, and although the magnificent limewood carvings in the saloon are attributed by family tradition to Grinling Gibbons,

much of the interior work was done by local craftsmen.

The entrance to Lyme Park – off the A6 at Disley – is at the approach to suburban Stockport, but the estate lies wholly in the National Park and its deer park stretches back on to the moors.

Macclesfield

Map Ref: 80SJ9273

An ancient market town on the lower, western slopes of the Pennines, Macclesfield has little to show from its earliest history, but the town turned in 1756 to the silk industry, gradually replacing Derby as the national centre of the trade. The last handloom weaver retired in 1981 when the firm of Cartwright & Sheldon closed down, but Paradise Mill – in which it was housed – has re-opened as a working museum. It is within five minutes' walk of the Heritage Centre in Roe Street.

East of the town centre the A537 Buxton road climbs steadily on to the moors, passing at 750ft Eddisbury Park Field – 16 acres of park-like meadow that is owned by the National Trust and which affords marvellous views across the Cheshire Plain.

The wild country south of the A537, from Walker Barn on the

National Park boundary to the county boundary beyond the Cat and Fiddle Inn, lay within medieval Macclesfield Forest. Now somewhat reduced in size, this survives as a managed coniferous forest containing a tiny chapel where a traditional rush-bearing ceremony is held in August. The Cat and Fiddle Inn, south of Shining Tor (1,834ft) was built in 1820 to catch the passing coach trade. One of England's most isolated inns, at 1,690ft it is also the second highest and often cut off in winter.

AA recommends:
Hotels: ◇ Ellesmere, Buxton Rd, 1-star, *tel.* (0625) 23791
Restaurants: ◇ Da Topo Gigio, 15 Church St, 1-fork, *tel.* (0625) 22231 ◇ Oliver's Bistro, 101 Chestergate, 1-fork, *tel.* (0625) 32003
Campsite: Capesthorne Hall, 2-pennants, *tel.* (0625) 861779 & 861584
Garage: ◇ Crossall Street (F & E Cadman), *tel.* (0625) 23036

Fishing at Ridgegate, Macclesfield

Matlock

Map Ref: 93SK3060

Which Matlock? There are eight, with eight other hamlets making up a sizable town which most people simply think of as Matlock – or perhaps Matlock Bath and Matlock Bridge. The oldest part is Old Matlock, where there can be found an 18th-century rectory next to Wheatsheaf Farm of 1681, which has the only mullioned and transomed windows in the place. Somebody found thermal water in 1698, and Matlock Bath was born as a spa of sorts. However, it was handicapped by having only 'a base, stony, mountainous road to it and no good accommodation when you are there'. Things have changed!

The building of the Old Bath Hotel in the 1730s and opening of what is now the A6 through Scarthin Nick in 1818, overcame such problems, and Matlock Bath achieved popularity. This was especially so with day trippers, who came first by canal to Cromford Wharf and then by train to Joseph Paxton's Swiss-chalet railway station, driving the long-stay visitor up the road to Smedley's Hydro (1853). For the next century this up-market hotel-cum-health farm dominated the town – as it does still as the headquarters of the Derbyshire County Council.

John Smedley, a dogmatic and eccentric industrialist who ran the Hydro (and Matlock), built himself the fairy-tale Riber Castle above the town. It is now a roofless shell in the grounds of Riber Wildlife Park, which specialises in European birds and animals – especially lynx. It is

also a Rare Breeds Survival Centre.

Matlock Bath is still the lively end, with lots happening in and around the Pavilion by the Derwent, including a good lead-mining museum and a tourist information centre. The whole town is worth seeing for the beauty of its setting in a deep gorge, best viewed from the cable cars which shuttle backwards and forwards high above. Architecturally, this is a Victorian town, in a fascinating area where there are caves in the hillsides – mostly old lead mines, possibly Roman – unexpected gardens on hilltops and excellent walking within easy reach.

AA recommends:

Hotels: New Bath, New Bath Rd, 3-star, *tel.* (0629) 583275 (2m S A6)
Riber Hall, Riber, 3-star country house hotel, *tel.* (0629) 582795
Red House, Old Rd, Darley Dale, 2-star, Country House Hotel *tel.* (0629) 734854 (2½m N A6)
Temple, Temple Walk, 2-star, *tel.* (0629) 583911
◇ Greyhound, Market Pl, Cromford, 1-star, *tel.* (062982) 2551 (2½m S on A5012)
Campsites: Packhorse Farm, Matlock Moor, 2-pennants, *tel.* (0629) 582781
Canada Farm, High Ln, Tansley, Venture Site, *tel.* (062 984) 385 (2m E off A615)
Self Catering: ◇ 10 North Street, Cromford, *tel.* (0629) 732221
◇ Bridge Cottage Flat, Bridge Cottage, Two Dales, *tel.* (0629) 732221
◇ Brook Cottage, Brookside, Two Dales, *tel.* (0629) 732221
◇ Chesterfield House, Chesterfield Rd, Two Dales *tel.* (0629) 732221
◇ Corner Cottage, Chesterfield Rd, Two Dales, *tel.* (0629) 732221
Guesthouses: Farley (farmhouse), *tel.* (0629) 582533
◇ Manor, Dethick (farmhouse), *tel.* (062984) 246
Packhorse, Matlock Moor (farmhouse), *tel.* (0629) 582781
Wayside, Matlock Moor (farmhouse), *tel.* (0629) 582967
Garages: Matlock Green Garage, Matlock Green, *tel.* (0629) 580480
Slaters, 50 Smedley St East, *tel.* (0629) 582101

Superb views of Matlock's gorge are afforded by a cable railway climbing to the Heights of Abraham (above)

Meltham

Map Ref: 83SE0910

Mills and moors dominate Meltham. The Victorian mills are massive, impressive and perhaps oppressive, while the moors lie at the end of every twisting, hilly street of this distinctively Pennine (rather than Peakland) woollen town. In both atmosphere and geography it is not far from J B Priestley's 'Bruddersford'.

The Carlile Institute of 1890 – including the Public Library – and the adjacent, slightly forbidding Town Hall are the most important public buildings in the main street. They are, however, less imposing than the great mill complex, with its tall red-brick building in the steep little valley below. Above – because everything in Meltham is either above or below – is what was originally an octagonal school building, 'built by subscription in 1823'. A later extension at the rear masks the shape from that side.

South-west of Meltham a minor road climbs to 1,640ft and joins the A635 for the crossing of Saddleworth Moor into Lancashire.

Miller's Dale

Map Ref: 92SK1373

This little settlement squeezed itself awkwardly into the narrow valley of the Wye – below the Midland Railway junction for Buxton on the main St Pancras to Manchester line – in the 1860s, providing housing for rail men and workers in various industries that had followed in the wake of the railway.

All these and the station, which also served as the village post office, have gone. The viaduct now carries the National Park's Monsal Trail footpath along the former railway track above the valley, the limeworks above the railway were spectacularly blown up in 1971, and their quarry is now a nature reserve. Four stone lime kilns dating from 1878 have been stabilised and are open to the public.

The hamlet takes its name from one of the best known of several beautiful dales accessible along the Wye to walkers. South of Buxton the A6 twists and turns alongside the river through Ashwood Dale, and is crossed in many places by the Midland railway line. Where the road leaves the river at the foot of Topley Pike the approach to Wye Dale is marred by a large quarry. Farther along there is the giant Tunstead Quarry – the largest in Europe and producer of exceptionally pure limestone –

which sprawls along Great Rocks Dale, a tributary valley.

From there to its confluence with the Derwent at Rowsley, however, the Wye is a gloriously clear and lovely river. The riverside path wanders through Chee, Miller's and Monsal Dales, providing some 6 miles of delightful walking. Chee Dale has a 50-acre nature reserve which includes Chee Tor, a prominent 300ft cliff with an exposed rock face, popular with climbers, above the river.

AA recommends:
Self Catering: ◇ The Dale House & Miller's Dale Cottage, *tel.* (0298) 871564

Miller's Dale from Monsal Head, showing the Wye's tree-fringed course through river-valley pastureland

Early Tourists

Despite its modern popularity, the Peak District received a very bad press at the hands of its earliest tourists. For instance, the 16th-century poet, Michael Drayton, described it as: '*A withered bedlam long, with bleared, waterish eyes; With many a bleak storm dimmed, which often to the skies; She cast, and oft to th' earth bowed down her aged head; Her meagre, wrinkled face being sullied still with lead.'*

Probably the first tourist guidebook to the Peak was written in long-winded Latin verse by Thomas Hobbes, the philosopher and tutor to the Cavendishes at Chatsworth. His *De Mirabilibus Pecci: Concerning the Wonders of the Peak in Darby-shire* published in 1636, listed seven 'wonders' which he had visited during a two-day ride.

They were: *Aedes, Mons, Barathrum, binus Fons, Antraque bina* – or a house (Chatsworth); a mountain

(Mam Tor); a chasm (Eldon Hole); two fountains (St Ann's Well in Buxton and the Ebbing and Flowing Well at Barmoor); and two caves (Poole's Cavern in Buxton and Peak

Even the dismissive 17th-century man of letters Daniel Defoe found that Eldon Hole justified its fame

Cavern, Castleton).

These wonders were later rehashed by Charles Cotton, squire of Beresford Hall in Dovedale and co-author with Izaac Walton of *The Compleat Angler*. However, even Cotton condemned Dovedale as 'this craggy, ill-contrived nook', while praising its trout-filled waters as 'the princess of rivers'.

The tour of the Seven Wonders of the Peak became an accepted and fashionable itinerary to those early visitors, including the redoubtable daughter of a Roundhead colonel, Celia Fiennes, who rode side-saddle through England in 1697. She wrote: 'All Derbyshire is full of steep hills, and nothing but the peakes of hills as thick as one by another is seen in most of the County which are very steepe which makes travelling tedious, and the miles long, you see neither hedge not tree but only low drye stone walls round some ground, else its only hills and dales as thick as you can imagine.'

Edward Browne, Norfolk-born son of Sir Thomas Browne, in his *Journal of a Tour in Derbyshire* (1662) found it a 'strange, mountainous, misty, moorish, rocky, wild country', while the cynical journalist and author, Daniel Defoe, was even more scathing of this 'howling wilderness'. 'This, perhaps, is the most desolate, wild and abandoned country in all England', he suggested in his *Tour Through the Whole Island of Great Britain* (1726) – adding that he found the inhabitants 'a rude boorish kind of people'. He poured scorn on the 'Wonders' of Hobbes and Cotton, dismissing all but Eldon Hole and Chatsworth, 'one a wonder of nature, the other of art'.

Later Romantics, like Lord Byron and John Ruskin, helped to develop the national taste for wild scenery. Byron claimed: 'there are things in Derbyshire as noble as in Greece or Switzerland', while Ruskin called the county 'a lovely child's alphabet; an alluring first lesson in all that is admirable'.

An 18th-century portrayal of the underground river in Peak Cavern

Monyash

Map Ref: 92SK1566

A bed of clay about 100yds square probably explains why Monyash is isolated in a slight bowl some 1,000ft up on the limestone uplands. For at the junction of the clay and limestone rose 23 springs which were retained in five natural meres on the impervious deposits. Fere Mere, the sole survivor but once the village's source of drinking water, stands within a stone enclosure built to deter cattle and close to the central cross-roads. Near by is a well that is dressed annually, probably as a thanksgiving for the water.

The market cross on the green has a medieval base and is the only indication – apart, perhaps, from the size of the church – that Monyash received a charter for a market in 1340. This plugged a 'trade gap' between Hartington and Bakewell. A village market is now held on the green on the two summer bank holidays.

A village so isolated had to be self-supporting, and the industries of Monyash have included a flint-tool 'factory' in prehistoric times, candle making, rope making, building meres for the farms around (redundant and fast disappearing since the belated arrival of piped water on these uplands), quarrying and lead mining – as evidenced by the mine hillocks littering the local fields. The 17th-century Bull's Head is the sole remaining of five village pubs.

Monyash was a Quaker stronghold in the late 18th century, but the movement has faded here, like the industries and the Barmote Court which used to meet to adjudicate in lead-mining disputes occurring the immediate area.

Monyash villagers once relied solely on Fere Mere (top) for drinking water. Ashford Marble, quarried near by, was first inlaid (above) in 1835

Among many excellent walks around the village, the most popular is down the River Lathkill, which in winter rises in a cave south east of the village just beyond the disused Ricklow Quarry. This one-time source of Ashford Marble (see page 33) is below Parson Tor, where a Monyash vicar fell to his death in 1776. In dry spells the river may rise much lower down its bed, near Over Haddon.

New Mills

Map Ref: 86SK0085

The new mill (just one) was built on the River Sett for grinding corn, around 1750, in the hamlet of Ollerset – one of several tiny settlements sited between Kinder Scout and the Goyt and once known collectively as Middlecale.

Ollerset and neighbouring Beard, Thornsett and Whittle were grouped together as a single township that came to be known as New Mills, which was adopted as the official name of a parish formed

in 1884. Soon there developed a town dominated by new cotton mills, some of which and their chimneys survive – along with spiky churches, solid Nonconformist chapels and rows of dark gritstone cottages which give the place its Lowry look. What really catches the eye is the deep gorge of the Goyt winding through the town centre, the splendid array of stone viaducts and bridges which span it, and the splendour of the brooding hills all around.

Among those hills to the north lies the tiny but beautiful hamlet of Rowarth. A footpath running north from there passes in less than a mile near a pair of round pillars set in a rock. Maps call them Robin Hood's Picking Rods, and tradition has it that they were used for bending and stringing bows. No better suggestion has been forthcoming, but they may have connections with the Basingwerk Abbey monks, the Monks Road being fairly near.

For those who prefer walking on the level, New Mills is at the western end of the Sett Trail from Hayfield, and indeed at the end of the river which here joins the Goyt.

AA recommends:
Garage: New Mills Motor Body Repairs, 84 Albion Rd, *tel.* (0663) 43040

Over Haddon

Map Ref: 92SK2066

The alphabetical accident which places Over Haddon next to New Mills serves to emphasise the enormous variety of Peak scenery, because no two places could provide a greater contrast. Over Haddon seems to float among the clouds when seen from the terraced garden of Haddon Hall, in the manor of Nether Haddon, and is a typical rural village of the limestone plateau. Its site at 800ft above sea level gives excellent views – especially south across Lathkill Dale to the tower of Youlgreave Church and the moors of Harthill and Gratton beyond.

Yet Over Haddon has an industrial past, with the relics of its lead mines still visible in the dale. The ruins of Mandale Mine's pumping house are down there among the thick foliage. So too is the leat (channel) which took water from a weir to turn the wheels of the Mandale and the Lathkill Dale mines, and the pillars of an aqueduct which carried it across the river. Close by are the remains of Carter's corn mill, but there is no trace – and never was – of the 'gold' which nearly turned Over Haddon into a mini-Klondike in the 1850s. It turned out to be iron pyrites, also known as fools gold.

Facing Over Haddon on the opposite rim of the Dale is Meadow Place Grange, one of a number of local monastic farms that were once at the heart of immense sheep runs. John Bright, of 19th-century Anti-Corn League fame, spent his honeymoon at One Ash Grange in a tributary valley called Cales Dale, higher upstream. One Ash belonged to the Cistercian house of Roche Abbey in Yorkshire.

In very dry weather the River Lathkill emerges from a long way down its true course, often necessitating the rescue of fish from the upper reaches. Repairs by Peak Park Conservation volunteers have been carried out on the bed and banks of the river to prevent this.

Downstream from Over Haddon, the Nature Conservancy Council in 1972 established the Peak's first National Nature Reserve, in mainly ash and elm woodland. It features a variety of shrubs, including the rare mezereon.

Parwich

Map Ref: 95SK1854

A mile inside the south-eastern corner of the Peak Park is Parwich, which sits pleasantly around and above a green in an area where the limestone uplands drop to the valley of Bradbourne Brook. Parwich Hall, standing commandingly above the village and digging its back into a sharply-rising hillside, is conspicuous for being of brick in a mainly stone-built village. As it was completed in 1747 – the same year as similarly brick-built Great Longstone Hall – suspicions of rivalry must be aroused.

On Parwich Moor above the village are more than 70 embanked circles of varying sizes and unknown function. They probably date from the Bronze Age, but do not seem to be funerary.

Parwich church is Victorian but retains from an earlier building a fine Norman tympanum over the north doorway. Alsop en le Dale lies 3 miles west and is at the start of various footpaths leading to Mill Dale, at the northern end of Dovedale. Its small church has a Norman nave and an interesting south doorway of that period. Ballidon, one mile east of Parwich, has an even smaller chapel sited in a field. This has much early-Norman work that was regrettably over-restored in 1882. The tiny village itself is completely overwhelmed by a large quarry and its attendant works.

A minor road from Parwich heads north to Pikehall, an agricultural hamlet which may have been more important in coaching days. The road passes close to Minninglow, capped at about 1,200ft by a few dying beech trees around the remains of several Neolithic chambered tombs.

From Minninglow car park, on the High Peak Trail, runs the 4-mile circular Roystone Grange Archaeological Trail. Using the former railway track, fields and farm tracks, this passes the remains of a medieval farm – of which the dairy has been excavated – plus a 'fossil' Roman field system, traces of a Roman manor house and farm buildings, and evidence of later quarrying and mining. Trail booklets are available from information centres and elsewhere, but shops in the immediate area are rarer than ancient remains.

AA recommends:
Self Catering: ◇ New Inns Holiday Cottages, Alsop-en-le-Dale, *tel.* (033527) 203

The River Lathkill from medieval Conksbury Bridge at Over Haddon – 3 miles from its source

Peak Forest

Map Ref: 87SK1179

Nothing could be more misleading than the name of this village, which shelters in a dip on the A623 road. Apart from a healthy clump of trees acting as a wind-break around the church, the landscape is almost bare. It seems to have been that way for a long time, for this part of the High Peak Forest was called *Campagna* – meaning 'open country' – and probably had few trees even before lead smelting and the Civil War took their toll.

Swainmotes (Forest Courts) were held here in Chamber Farm, which was rebuilt in the 18th century, and were conducted by the Steward of the Forest with not fewer than 20 foresters. They ensured that forest laws were enforced justly and without undue harshness.

The church given by the 7th Duke of Devonshire in 1877 retains the unusual dedication to King Charles the Martyr of its more interesting predecessor, which was built by Christian, Countess of Devonshire in 1657. She intended it as a private chapel within the royal forest and outside the jurisdiction of a bishop. It was also outside the law in being raised during the Commonwealth ban on church-building. The incumbent – in full, 'The Principal Officer and Judge in Spiritualities in the Peculiar Court of Peak Forest' – took advantage of his unusual position to make money from marriages. These he conducted without question at any time of day or night as a kind of Peakland 'Gretna Green', until Lord Hardwicke's Marriage Act of 1753 restricted him to daylight hours only. Even then, clandestine marriages continued until 1804.

About a mile north of Peak Forest is Eldon Hole, the so-called 'Bottomless Pit' and one of the traditional Seven Wonders of the Peak. It is actually 200ft deep, and one of only two good-sized swallow holes in the National Park. The other is 495ft Giant's Hole, situated on the other side of Eldon near the foot of Rushup Edge.

Penistone

Map Ref: 85SE2403

Quietly flows the Don past – rather than through – Penistone before entering the industrial sprawl of Sheffield, and the market town itself stands handsomely above the river in two shades of gritstone. Its mainly 14th-century, battlemented church appears particularly sombre from without – probably the result of centuries of smoke pollution, much reduced in recent years – but not even a coating of soot can hide its intrinsic attractiveness.

Between the church in its pleasant churchyard at the top of town and the long main street curving gently down under one of many railway bridges before dropping into the valley is a former market hall in the Classical style – now used for various other purposes.

Penistone is a musical town – as Pennine towns tend to be – with a brass band, majorettes and an annual 'sing' which started in 1885 and usually takes place in late June. It also has its Penistone Players, a still-active cinema, and not the least of its attractions, good free parking.

The approach up the valley from Oxspring is enhanced by good stone viaducts, if marred by ugly black electricity pylons. The countryside north and west is magnificent.

It is unlikely that trees were ever a major feature at Peak Forest

Rowsley

Map Ref: 93SK2566

'The scenery is varied and beautiful – a combination of wood and water, and hill, dale and meadow.' No change has affected that 1895 description of Great Rowsley, where the A6 enters the National Park from the south across a 15th-century Derwent bridge that was widened in 1925 and stands just upstream of the river's confluence with the Wye. It is a village of gracious houses – almost all owned by the Duke of Rutland.

The Peacock, built as a private house in 1652, became an inn around 1828 and was described 20 years later as 'the beau ideal of an English country hostelry'. Then as now it was much favoured by anglers. The nearby Grouse and Claret, originally the Station Hotel, now correctly carries the sign of a fishing-fly – not the bird and drink that an earlier signwriter painted.

Caudwell's Mill on the Wye was operated by water-power from 1874 to 1978, and having been restored by volunteers is again using roller-milling machinery installed early this century to produce traditional wholemeal flour.

Little Rowsley, a railway colony of mainly red-brick houses, stands on the Chatsworth road east of the River Derwent and outside the National Park. Although the railway and its depot closed in the 1960s, Paxton's delightful station of 1849 survives on a small industrial estate. In 1986 the second station was re-erected at the Peak Rail Centre in Buxton.

AA recommends:
Hotel: Peacock, 3-star, *tel.* (0629) 733518
Self Catering: ◇ Greystones, Church Ln (flat), *tel.* (0629) 733518
◇ Rose Cottage, Church Ln, *tel.* (0629) 733518

Corn is ground for wholemeal flour at the restored Caudwell's Mill

Elaborate ornamentation on Rowsley's Peacock Hotel, once a private house

Rudyard

Map Ref: 80SJ9558

Less than half a mile west of the A523 and 3 miles north of Leek is Rudyard, a Victorian lakeside resort encircled by hills. Rudyard 'Lake' is actually a reservoir that was constructed in 1799 to feed the Caldon Canal. From 1845 the North Staffordshire Railway Company, which had acquired the

Rudyard Lake reservoir, a beautiful venue for water sports and rambles

canal, developed the reservoir and old village as a pleasure resort. Excursion trains from Leek arrived at Rudyard every 15 minutes during Bank Holiday peak periods. On one day in 1877 20,000 people went there to see Captain Webb swim.

Among those with particular reason to remember Rudyard were John Lockwood Kipling and his wife Alice, for it was there that they became engaged. In gratitude they named their son Rudyard, who later became the famous author.

Sailing and coarse fishing are available on the lake, and the 4-mile walk round it includes on the west shore a section of the Staffordshire Way footpath that will eventually extend for 90 miles between Mow Cop and Kinver Edge. The road west from the lake goes to Horton, which has some interesting old houses and a mainly 16th-century church containing Wedgwood family monuments. The main road north passes through Rushton Spencer, where a fine railway station has been converted into a private house, and a hilltop church of many styles is sometimes known as 'The Chapel in the Wilderness'.

AA recommends:

Self Catering: ◇ Reacliffe Cottage, *tel.* (053833) 276

Guesthouses: ◇ Barnswood, Rushton Spencer (farmhouse), *tel.* (02606) 261 ◇ Fairboroughs (farmhouse), *tel.* (02606) 341

Sheldon

Map Ref: 92SK1768

A former lead-mining village, Sheldon clings to a steep hillside just below the rim of the limestone uplands at 1,000ft, its single street bordered by wide strips of green. The farmhouses and cottages behind the green date mainly from the 18th century, a time when its mining industry was flourishing.

The plateau above the village is dotted with prehistoric monuments and the remnants of lead mining, but the dominant feature is Magpie Mine – last worked (unsuccessfully) in 1958. Its buildings date from a century earlier, and it has records going back to 1739. Said to be both cursed and haunted, the mine was stabilised in the 1970s and is probably the best preserved surviving in Britain. Visiting parties can be arranged through the Peak District Mining Museum at Matlock Bath, and it serves as a field centre for the Peak District Mines Historical Society.

West across the open moor is Flagg, a remote hamlet with a handsome Elizabethan Hall. The High Peak Hunt point-to-point races are held annually on Easter Tuesday at the edge of the parish, near the A515 road and close to the picturesque Bull I' Th' Thorn Inn – an interesting building which is believed to date from 1472.

Stanton in Peak

Map Ref: 93SK2464

Long, steep, single-street hillside villages are numerous in Peakland, and Stanton in Peak, on the northern scarp of Stanton Moor, is typical – although the street curves more than others, and has numerous tributary alleyways and secluded courtyards.

The initials WPT over cottage doorways stand for William Paul Thornhill of Stanton Hall, which is still occupied by his Davie-Thornhill descendants, but out of sight behind a high wall near the church. His family gave the church to the village in 1839, along with a bronze holy-water stoup dated 1596. 'The Flying Childers' Inn is named after a successful racehorse owned by the 4th Duke of Devonshire.

Above the village is Stanton Moor, an isolated island of gritstone rising to 1,096ft from a limestone sea. On this long plateau are more than 70 barrows and cairns that were all excavated this century by a father and son team, the late J C and J P Heathcote of Birchover. Perhaps the most interesting feature is the stone circle known as The Nine Ladies. The solitary King's Stone standing near by may be connected with it, but other upright

Sunset softens the hard, gritstone edges of Stanton Moor, where mysterious barrows and standing stones are scattered among rock pillars formed naturally by erosion.
Inset: prehistoric cairns litter the moor

stones on the moor are natural survivors from eroded millstone grit. The tower on Stanton Moor Edge was erected in 1832 in honour of Earl Grey's involvement in the passing of the Reform Act.

AA recommends:
Self Catering: ◇ Woodview Cottage, *tel.* (062986) 358

Stocksbridge

Map Ref: 85SK2798

'How green was my valley once', one is tempted to quote as Deepcar merges into Stocksbridge without any noticeable change in the 2-mile dark ribbon of houses on either side of the A616(T). The odd thing is that the valley of the River Porter – or Little Don – is still green on its higher northern slopes above the great steel works that frowns across at Stocksbridge. Even on the southern side above the road the steep hillside has been landscaped and converted into a pleasing stretch

of public park, with seats where one can ruminate on this strange juxtaposition of ugliness and beauty.

The ugliness is only skin-deep. A mile north or south of the V-shaped valley is open moorland; 2 miles south is the National Park boundary, and the wilderness of Broomhead Moor and Bradfield Moor. Even west the Stocksbridge sprawl halts abruptly at the dam wall of Underbank Reservoir, beyond which is a long, open, scenic stretch of road through Langsett to Holmfirth.

Stocksbridge is the last fling of Sheffield and the steel country. Two miles north east in idyllic surroundings by the Don can be seen where and how it all began – at Wortley Top Forge (open on Sundays), which is typical of the little ironworks that laid the foundations of Sheffield's wealth back in monastic times.

Relying at first on just a few workers – perhaps only one family – and on the power of hill streams, they sprang up all around Sheffield. Wortley Top, which may have been working in medieval times, definitely was in 1695 and continued in production until 1929. Visitors to the forge today see the results of rebuilding in 1713, with both machinery and structure virtually unchanged since then.

Stoney Middleton

Map Ref: 89SK2375

Stony is certainly is, with great natural walls of white limestone rising sheer from the floor of Middleton Dale and blocking the sunlight from the A623 road. Higher up the dale are two large quarries, and all around are disused ones – as well as traces of disused lead mines. The numerous limekilns have gone, however, and with them the 'sulphur smells and thick smoke'

Springs beneath this bath house may have been used by the Romans

that hung over both valley and village in the 18th century.

Stoney Middleton is now a clean, pleasant village of character, especially away from the main road around The Nook – a charming square where two wells are dressed in July to August. Close by is a rare octagonal church with a lantern storey that was grafted on to a Perpendicular tower in 1759. The Jacobean Hall behind was the home of the Denmans – mostly distinguished surgeons, apart from one notable exception who became Lord Chief Justice in 1832. He may have built the bath-house whose ruins stand over thermal springs which the Romans may have used.

The present main road, still called New Road, was laid out by the turnpike trustees in 1840. The octagonal tollhouse of that date – a listed building – is now a chip shop. Higher up is Lover's Leap, so called since 1762 when a jilted girl called Hannah Badderley tried to end it all by jumping from a high rock. Her voluminous skirt opened like a parachute and caught on brambles protruding from a ledge, where she hung suspended for a while before rolling gently and only slightly injured into a saw-pit.

Stoney Middleton was once a boot- and shoe-making centre, and a surviving firm operates from a former corn mill. The largest source of employment is, however, the fluorspar industry – based 1,000ft up on the moors above the village. Nearly threequarters of Britain's fluorspar – used in the production of steel, chemicals, ceramics and aluminium – is produced from a strip of limestone upland that extends south from the Hope Valley almost to Matlock and Wirksworth, but is little more than a single mile wide.

Climbing Country

Frowning down on the broad shale valley of the Derwent for about 15 miles from Outer Edge in the north to Harland Edge in the south are the famous Peakland Eastern Edges.

These precipitous, castellated walls of gritstone, up to 60ft high in places like Stanage Edge near Hathersage, attract rock climbers from all over Britain. The firm, abrasive qualities of Peakland grit are highly-regarded in the climbing world, and the severity of the routes which have been led on it is in a class out of all proportion to the modest elevations.

The edges are the eroded remains of a millstone grit cap, formed by the deltas of Carboniferous Age rivers, which once covered the limestone of the White Peak.

Many of the finest climbers Britain has produced first made their names on these rock walls, so close to the great northern cities from where they came. Men like Joe Brown and the late Don Whillans from Manchester took the sport of rock climbing to new extremes in the 1950s and '60s, and many of their pioneering routes are still held in awe by climbers today.

Stanage is still the Mecca for the gritstone rock athlete, and on a sunny weekend, the four miles of crags can be festooned with brightly-coloured ropes like streamers at a party. The names given to routes like the Right and Left Unconquerables have long since proved inaccurate, and today over 500 other climbs exist along the weathered ramparts.

Over on the opposite side of the National Park, the edges of the western fringe are more shattered but offer climbing routes every bit as severe in places like the Roaches, Hen Cloud and Windgather Rocks. Don Whillans' challenging overhang route, The Sloth (so-called because of the length of time spent hanging upside down) remains designated a classic 'hard very severe'.

Rock climbing began in the Peak District around the turn of the century with pioneers like J W Puttrell investigating the edges for their climbing potential for the first time. It could be said the sport was born here, although Lake District afficionados would probably dispute it. No one could deny though that this is where it blossomed, and several of its best climbers went on to become conquerors of Alpine and Himalayan giants, including Everest.

In later years, attention has increasingly been switched to the even longer and more exposed routes on the smooth limestone crags of the dales, which take the sport of rock climbing into ever greater extremes of athleticism and demand greater use of artificial aids in the conquest of new challenges.

For those who want nothing more than a pleasant stroll with outstanding views, the paths along the tops of the edges provide a breathtaking promenade – with the added interest of the remains of the forgotten industry of millstone making at their foot, and the antics of the climbers for company.

A millstone grit edge at Curbar

Taddington

Map Ref: 92SK1471

As the A6 road climbs sinuously through Taddington Dale from Ashford its steep gradient is disguised by numerous bends and the thick woodlands on either side. Above the tree-line on the bare plateau it avoids the long, rising main street of Taddington by following one of the earliest Peakland village bypasses.

Taddington is large, its cottages small and simple and its rather grand church commandingly sited at the top of the village. On the strength of prospering wool and lead trades, some splendid churches were built or rebuilt in the 14th century, with nearby Tideswell the supreme example. Taddington is smaller and less ambitious.

From the church, a footpath running west over Taddington Moor to Chelmorton reaches 1,438ft before, after 1½ miles, passing close to Five Wells Tumulus – the highest megalithic tomb in England. On private land, the mound has eroded away to expose two burial chambers of limestone slabs. Inside were 12 inhumations, flint tools and scraps of pottery. The name is significant, for the numerous springs rising hereabouts account for the wealth of tumuli at this height – and also probably for the siting of Taddington.

North of the bypass is evidence of Celtic or early-Saxon terrace cultivation at Priestcliffe, in the form of stepped 'lynchets'.

Taxal and Whaley Bridge

Map Ref: 86SK0079

Whaley Bridge is a small town, while Taxal consists merely of a church, the Chimes of Taxal Inn (formerly the Royal Oak) and perhaps a dozen gritstone houses among trees on the west bank of the Goyt. Taxal, however, is the senior partner by many centuries. Its church remains the parish church

Thick, broadleafed woodland escorts the A6 through Taddington Dale

and its large churchyard the official cemetery for Whaley Bridge – which was a cotton-weaving town and is now concerned with engineering and clothing.

Although a boundary change in 1936 transferred Taxal from Cheshire to Derbyshire, it remains in the Diocese of Chester and Province of York – except for the hamlet of Fernilee across the Goyt, which is in Derby Diocese in Canterbury Province but regards Taxal as its parish church. The large parish extends virtually from Lyme Park in the north to the Cat and Fiddle in the south, and from Rainow on the west to Chapel-en-le-Frith in the east.

Windgather Rocks, overlooking Taxal in the west, is a favourite training-ground for rock climbers. Beyond that is the little village of Kettleshulme, where candlewicks were made until 1937. The Bow Stones, a mile north west of Kettleshulme, may have been used for stringing bows – though a rival theory is that they mark the boundary of Macclesfield Forest.

South of Kettleshulme at Saltersford is the isolated Jenkin Chapel of 1733, which has

domestic windows and chimney, and a saddleback tower that was added in 1755. It also retains its original box pews, pulpit and reading desk. An open-air harvest-festival service is usually held there sometime in September.

The Cromford & High Peak Railway used to drop dramatically down an inclined plane and to its northern terminus at the Whaley Bridge basin on the Peak Forest Canal. The basin has now been well restored as a popular marina.

Tideswell

Map Ref: 88SK1575

Tideswell Church is often described as 'The Cathedral of the Peak'. The splendid cruciform building was erected between about 1300 and 1370, with just a short break immediately after the Black Death, so it is almost wholly in the Decorated style. Only the soaring and pinnacled west tower – which is in the then newly-fashionable Perpendicular style – and just a few hints of changing trends in the chancel are the exceptions.

The whole church is spacious and lofty, the tower arch and the east

Built almost entirely in the Decorated style, 14th-century Tideswell Church is a cathedral in everything but name

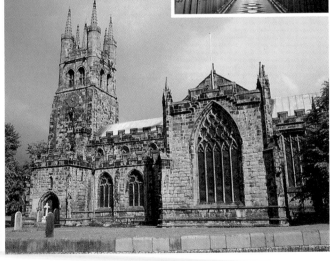

and west windows being exceptionally tall. Its chancel is rich in pre-Reformation tombs and brasses, and the building displays a wealth of wood carving – mainly 19th-century work by Suffolk carvers and local man Advent Hunstone, whose nephew continues the family tradition in the present century.

Tideswell is in fact a village of craftsmen, working on their own in buildings converted from other uses. This is apparent from the excellence of its well-dressing, which starts – along with the week-long wakes – on the Saturday which falls nearest St John the Baptist Day.

Architecturally the village tends to suffer by comparison with its glorious church, and so to be underrated. Exploration of its streets and alleyways is most rewarding, however, with many of the buildings revealing themselves as being older than they look.

The late 18th-century George Hotel – with its Venetian windows – and both Blake House and Eccles Hall are especially interesting. The gardens of 'Welyards' in Sherwood Road are frequently open and worth seeing, but it is a waste of time looking for the ebbing and flowing well, which ceased to do either when piped water arrived many years ago. It had been one of the traditional Seven Wonders of the Peak along with Chatsworth, Eldon Hole, St Anne's Well and Poole's Cavern, Buxton, Mam Tor and Peak Cavern.

Tideswell received a market charter in 1250, flourished in the wool and lead trades during the 14th century – which explains the lavishness of the church – then declined to village status and, luckily, became too poor to update its church. North west of Tideswell, in the hamlet of Wheston, is a small but complete 15th-century village cross, a dilapidated and 'haunted' 16th- and 17th-century hall and several interesting old farmhouses. Farther south is Monks Dale National Nature Reserve.

Tintwistle and Longdendale

Map Ref: 82SK0297

Tintwistle is another 'last outpost of civilisation' – the final link in a chain of 19th-century cotton towns and villages that began miles to the north west in central Lancashire, and petered out on the western boundary of the National Park where the wilderness of Longdendale begins. It was a small, gritstone village when the domestic cotton industry arrived in around 1750, then trebled its population between 1801 and 1851, when the first mills were built.

The mills have gone and the population is halved, but terraces of weavers' cottages survive in Higher Square, Lower Square and Chapel Brow at the older, unplanned eastern end of the village. There, from a sloping green 800ft above sea level, can be enjoyed an impressive view across Bottoms Reservoir to the encircling hills.

Bottoms is the lowest in a chain of five reservoirs, which with two more west of Tintwistle, were constructed for Manchester Corporation along the valley of Longdendale over a 30-year period from 1848. The work followed almost immediately after completion of the first two Woodhead tunnels on the Manchester to Sheffield section of what became the Great Central Line. During the operation some 32 died (mainly of cholera), and there were countless injuries. When a third tunnel opened in 1954 to take the newly-electrified line the first two were closed, though one was re-opened in the 1960s to take electric transmission lines and so avoid further scarring of the Longdendale landscape.

Since then the railway service has ended and the threat of a motorway through Longdendale has so far been averted, but the threat of a pumped storage plant at Robinson's Moss still hangs over this blemished but still wildly-beautiful valley. Walking in the surrounding hills is wonderful for experienced people with the right equipment – including the Park Board's pamphlet *Walks Around Longdendale*.

The Pennine Way drops down to Crowden Youth Hostel – overlooking Torside Reservoir, where there is sailing – then climbs north again to Black Hill (1,908ft).

Longdendale, from the village cross and green high up in Tintwistle

Tissington and Fenny Bentley

Map Ref: 95SK1752

Many people consider Tissington to be the most beautiful village in the National Park, and well-dressing enthusiasts revere it as the birthplace of the traditional craft.

It has everything the tourist desires except an inn – a Norman church on a mound facing a splendid Jacobean manor house, ducks sailing serenely on the village mere, cheerful limestone houses set back behind wide strips of green and five attractive wells which – with a children's well – are dressed on Ascension Day.

The whole village has been carefully managed by the Fitzherbert family since the reign of Elizabeth I. From the original manor house on the site of an Iron Age fort next to the church, they moved across the road to their newly-built Tissington Hall in about

Tissington Trail follows a level railway trackbed and is an excellent foot or bicycle route into the Peak countryside

1610. They extended the hall in Georgian times, then again early this century, and rebuilt most of the

other houses in the traditional local style between about 1830 and 1860. The church was perhaps over-restored in 1854.

Fenny Bentley straddles the winding A515 road 2 miles away and is the Peak Park's southernmost

Farming in the Peak

Man has been farming in the Peak District for well over 5,000 years, and the landscape admired by visitors today is largely the creation of successive generations of farmers.

Forest clearance began in Mesolithic times, on the now bleak, open moorlands of the Dark Peak and rolling upland pastures of the White Peak limestone plateau. In fact, it is probably only in the rocky gritstone cloughs and crags of the limestone dales which are inaccessible to grazing animals that a truly natural landscape, untouched by man, can be found today.

Farming is still the most important single industry in the Peak District, although the number of people employed by it is decreasing through mechanisation and the demise of many small family farms. In an upland area like the Peak District, the most typical form of farming is pastoral, and livestock enterprises predominate. Dairying and sheep are most common on the limestone plateau, although on the lower slopes – especially around Bakewell – an increasing amount of land has been turned over to arable crops, particularly the alien mustard-yellow of oilseed rape.

Concrete-lined dewponds, locally known as meres, have been constructed over the years to catch the precious rainwater and to provide water for stock. Perhaps the most distinctive feature are the miles and miles of drystone walls which spread over the gently-swelling contours like a net, keeping the stock from straying. Most were constructed by the Enclosure Acts of the late 18th and early 19th centuries, when open moorland was parcelled off.

Recent research has shown, however, that some walls are much older than this, and may go back to medieval or even Roman times. Certainly, sheep and cattle have been kept on these sweet limestone pastures for many centuries, and although the traditional economy of mining and farming is seldom practised today, they remain two of the most important sources of employment.

On the Dark Peak moorlands, sheep reign supreme and share their lofty heather-clad pastures with the red grouse, which are shot annually after the 'Glorious 12th' of August. The Peak District is the home of two specialist breeds of mountain sheep bred to withstand the rigours of the harsh Dark Peak winters. They are the polled, speckle-faced Derbyshire Gritstone, originally known as the Dale O'Goyt, and the large Roman-nosed Whitefaced Woodland, from the Woodlands Valley in the north of the district.

Drystone walling has been called a dying art, but there are many seasoned practitioners around who can still build a mortarless wall which will stand for two centuries. So important a feature are these lasting monuments that the National Park authority has actually paid farmers in a couple of villages to ensure their upkeep and maintenance.

Farming has always been an important part of the Peak economy, alongside mining

village. Its smattering of Midland-clay brick houses is scattered among more numerous stone ones, and although the village has not had a resident squire for three centuries its interesting medieval church is still dominated by the Beresfords – one-time chief family. Thomas, who survived Agincourt and a further 58 years, shares in effigy with his wife an impressive alabaster tomb-chest.

Their descendants attend an annual reunion of the Beresford Family Society, and parts of their

Stately old 15th-century manor house with a fortified pele tower – possibly a gatehouse – at Fenny Bentley

medieval moated manor house are embodied in Cherry Orchard Farm. A massive square tower, like a defensive Northumbrian pele tower, may have been part of a gatehouse.

Tissington Trail crosses Bentley Hill between the villages on its way to Tissington's former railway station, where there is a car park, picnic site and refreshments. Near by are excellent examples of the old open-field farming system.

AA recommends:
Hotel: Bentley Brook Inn, Fenny Bentley, 2-star, *tel.* (033529) 278
Campsites: Highfield Caravan Park, Highfield Farm, 3-pennants, *tel.* (033529) 228
Bank Top Farm, 1-pennant, *tel.* (033529) 250
Self Catering: ◊ Drysdale, Fenny Bentley, *tel.* (033525) 214
Guesthouse: Bent, Tissington (farmhouse), *tel.* (033525) 214

Warslow and the Elkstones

Map Ref: 94SK0858

For dramatic effect, these two places are best seen in reverse order. A minor road running south from the Mermaid Inn seems to drop through a hole in the moors, and the houses of Upper Elkstone cling grimly to the steep, spiral route. Unexpectedly simple, the towerless and aisleless village church is on a level platform. Behind its round-headed sash windows are box pews,

a gallery, a two-decker pulpit and the Royal Arms of George III – all dating from 1786. It also has a Morris window of 1922.

At the foot of the hill are a few farmhouses that make up Lower Elkstone in the remote green valley of Warslow Brook. It is a different world from both the bare moorlands above and the populous Potteries 15 miles away.

By comparison Warslow seems large and sophisticated, but is in fact a pleasantly leafy, stone-built estate village with a church of 1820 provided by Sir George Crewe – of Calke Abbey. Its chancel was added in 1908, and it features much 20th-century stained glass by Morris & Co. Sir George built Warslow Hall, 1½ miles outside the village on the Longnor road, as a shooting box.

Waterhouses

Map Ref: 94SK0850

A footpath along the Hamps and Manifold valleys starts from a car park on the north side of the A523 Ashbourne to Leek road, which keeps company with the Hamps part of the way through this straggling village – once a terminus of the now-defunct Manifold Valley Light Railway.

South at Cauldon is a large and too-prominent cement works close to Cauldon Low, a hill which has been almost munched away by quarrying. Some of the disused quarries provide interesting rockface profiles, visible from an award-winning craft centre and health-food restaurant housed in a former school in Cauldon Lowe village. Away from this small industrial belt the surrounding countryside is splendid and rewards exploration.

Wildboarclough

Map Ref: 90SJ9868

The last wild boar was hunted to extinction here in the 15th century, and the last of three mid 18th-

century mills that turned the village into an outpost of the Macclesfield silk industry – and later made carpets exhibited at the Great Exhibition of 1851 – was demolished in 1958. The only road through the clough below Shutlingsloe (1,659ft) is still attended by its chain of little waterfalls on Clough Brook, however, and Wildboarclough is still an attractive little village in gorgeously remote countryside.

James Brindley, later of canal fame, installed the machinery at the village's first silk mill while apprenticed to Abraham Bennett of Sutton, near Macclesfield. Although the mill has gone, the administrative building has survived.

Clough Brook turned the wheels of a vanished paper mill at Allgreave, just before its confluence with the Dane – which powered another paper mill at Wincle, between Back Dane and the attractive hamlet of Danebridge. At Gradbach, one mile up the Dane before its junction with the brook, a former 18th-century silk mill (rebuilt after a fire in 1785 and converted into a saw mill by Sir John Harpur Crewe in the 1870s), has been converted recently into a Youth Hostel.

A track running west from Gradbach ends close to Lud's Church, which is an extraordinary cleft between walls of rock 20ft apart on the edge of Back Forest. It was a secret place or worship for Wycliff's Lollards in the 14th century, taking its name from – apparently – from Walter de Lud-Auk and setting part of the scene, according to recent research, for the famous medieval poem *Sir Gawain and the Green Knight*. Lud's Church has been identified as the Green Chapel, and the medieval hunting lodge of Swythamley Hall as the site of the Green Knight's castle. Swythamley Hall was rebuilt by the Brocklehurst family during the mid 19th century.

This beautifully restored 18th-century building at Gradbach once housed silk-milling machines

Winster

Map Ref: 93SK2460

Winster may have lost its town status and weekly market, but it retains its dignity and urbanity. It has also kept its charming market hall, the most conspicuous of its buildings because it protrudes into Main Street. The 16th-century ground floor was once open, as at Chipping Campden, Ross-on-Wye and Bakewell, but the space between the pointed arches has been filled in. The brick upper storey, added a century later, houses an information centre and shop belonging to the National Trust – who bought it in 1906 as its first purchase in Derbyshire or the Peak. It is open at weekends and bank holidays from April to September.

Other imposing houses, nearly all with three storeys, can be seen in Main Street. Those on East Bank and West Bank date mostly from the 18th-century heyday of local lead mining. The double-gabled Dower House, at the west end of Main Street, is a century earlier. Less dignified but no less endearing are the little alleyways or 'ginnels', running off Main Street and up the sheltering cliffside.

A bell summons Winster housewives to an annual Shrove Tuesday pancake race, there is a village market on summer bank holidays and a week of Wakes festivities at the end of June – as well as morris dancing at various times of the year.

Just out of the village on the B5056, near the top of West Bank, is the Miner's Standard Inn – which takes its name from the standard dish used by miners for measuring lead ore (see Wirksworth). Appropriately, the area is riddled with old lead-mine shafts and hillocks. A mile east of Winster is the pretty limestone village of Wensley, on a hillside where the B5057 drops from Wensley Dale to cross the River Derwent at Darley Bridge.

Wirksworth

Map Ref: 81SK2854

Daniel Defoe in about 1720 saw Wirksworth as 'a kind of market for lead: the like not known anywhere else that I know of. . . .' – but the lead industry died, and Wirksworth almost expired with it. Now, thanks to a Civic Trust Project and a lot of hard work by The Derbyshire Historic Buildings Trust and many other bodies, it has been reborn and seems destined to become an important tourist centre.

It has the natural advantage of a good position in a bowl of the hills at the head of the Ecclesbourne Valley, where a number of minor roads meet. Two of them curve uphill to meet by a crazily tilted

market place. It also has a minor part in literary history as the Snowfield of *Adam Bede*, and the home of author George Eliot's aunt, Elizabeth Evans – the model for Dinah Bede. Hers was the first house on the right as the town is entered by the Derby road.

The splendid church in a most charming circular mini-close is already a tourist attraction, mainly because of what is probably the Peak's earliest Christian monument – a coffin lid discovered in 1820 but dating from the late 7th century.

Moot Hall, which was rebuilt in 1812, is where the Barmote Court still meets twice annually to settle lead-mining disputes – as it is known to have done since 1266 and almost certainly has for much longer. A standard measuring dish holding 14 pints of ore and made in 1512 hangs on the wall.

Wirksworth dresses nine wells on late Spring Bank Holiday Saturday, which coincides with the annual Carnival. The annual ceremony of Clypping (embracing) the Church takes place on the Sunday after 8 September.

Middleton-by-Wirksworth, 1½ miles north-west, is a hillside quarrying village of character which has a huge and rare limestone mine.

Winster's charming market hall dates from the 16th and 17th centuries. Another reminder of times past are frequent displays of morris dancing at various times, celebrated in the illustration on a town pub sign

The famous Hopton Wood Marble (a form of limestone) from Middleton has been used in such buildings as Westminster Abbey, York Minster and the Houses of Parliament, and for headstones in war cemeteries. Above the village is Middleton Top Engine House, on the High Peak Trail. It has a beam engine built at the Ripley Butterley Works in 1829.

Wormhill

Map Ref: 91SK1274

Midway between Buxton and Tideswell and directly above Chee Dale, Wormhill is not so much a village as an extended collection of handsome old farmhouses climbing a minor road to more than 1,000ft at Wormhill Hill. On the road north to Hargatewall is Old Hall Farm, which dates from the 16th and 17th centuries and was probably a manor house before the present H-shaped hall was built at the foot of the hill in 1697. Behind the hall at a higher level is the church, which was rebuilt in 1864 and capped by a Rhineland-style tower – perhaps inspired by the Saxon helm-tower a long way south at Sompting in Sussex.

On the green in 1895 an ornate stone structure was erected round a well in rather belated memory of 'James Brindley, Civil Engineer, Born in this Parish AD 1716'. His cottage birthplace at Tunstead was demolished shortly after his death in 1772 because a persistent ash tree kept growing through the floor. His well is dressed annually on the Saturday falling before the late August Bank Holiday.

The views from Wormhill are spectacular, though to the west they are dominated by the quarries of Great Rocks Dale, which threaten to encroach into the parish within the next century.

Youlgreave

Map Ref: 92SK2164

There may be doubts about the spelling – more than 60 versions exist – but none at all about the charm of this extended linear village, which runs along a shelf of fairly level ground between the Bradford and Lathkill Rivers before they join. Behind the cottages on the south side of the long, narrow street (that has been called 'England's longest car park'), are pretty, private gardens that tumble down to the Bradford, which flows so close below the cliff as to be invisible from above. A road by the church and numerous alleyways and stone steps lead down to the river, which is spanned in quick succession by a packhorse bridge, a clapper bridge and a rather more modern road bridge.

The church juts out into the main street, and from some angles its splendid Perpendicular tower appears to block the roadway. Its wide nave is mainly Norman, as is the large tub-font with a rare

attached stoop for oil. Among an interesting collection of monuments is a mini-tomb and mini-effigy in alabaster to Thomas Cockayne, killed in a teenage brawl in 1488.

Near the church are some rather grand Georgian houses, while farther west is the Old Hall – a long, low, mullioned building that is typical of the White Peak and dated 1656. It may be older. Behind it, screened from the street, is the Old Hall Farm of around 1630. A marvellous, three-storey shop built for the local Co-operative Society in 1887 now serves as a Youth Hostel.

Facing it from the site of a Saxon cross is an oval gritstone water tank officially called The Conduit Head, and unofficially The Fountain. This was built in 1829 by the village's own water company to supply soft water to all who paid sixpence annually. The boon was celebrated by Youlgreave's first known well-dressing in 1829. It now dresses five wells to a remarkably high standard even compared with the superb showpieces for which other Peak villages are famous, and still operates

its own water-supply company.

East of the village the road drops to Alport, once a mill settlement making industrial use of the two rivers, but now a pretty little residential village much visited by artists. West along the river, where Bradford Dale becomes Middleton Dale, is Middleton-by-Youlgreave. Equally pretty, it is also exceptionally well-blessed with trees for the normally fairly unforested White Peak.

Lomberdale Hall, just outside the village, was the home of Thomas Bateman – the Victorian archaeologist of the area. His grave – appropriately surmounted by a Bronze Age urn – stands alone in a private field. He excavated over 500 barrows in 20 years, and the artefacts he discovered are exhibited mainly in Sheffield's interesting Western Park Museum.

AA recommends:
Guesthouse: Bulls Head, Church St (inn) *tel.* (0629) 636307
Garage: Peter Prince (Auto & Elec Eng), The Garage, *tel.* (0629) 636206

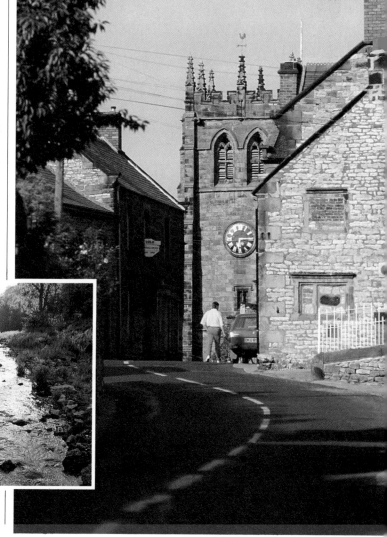

A sunny evening highlights the warm stone of Youlgreave Church, elegant counterpoint to nearby Bradford Dale

Directory

ANGLING

Famous for its fishing potential
from at least the days of Izaak
Walton and Charles Cotton – co-
authors of *The Compleat Angler* –
the Derbyshire Dales still hold and
fulfil the promise of fine sport in
their gin-clear rivers and streams.

However, the casual angler
should beware, for it is more than
likely that the fish belong to
somebody already. Most of the
really worthwhile waters in the area
have been reserved by local hotels
and clubs, while any that have not
are still under the control of the
Severn-Trent Water Authority and
cannot be fished without an official
licence from that body.

That also applies to the great
complexes of reservoirs in the
Derwent Valley – 504 acres of
water in the Ladybower alone –
that have achieved a maturity to
make them worthy of the game-
fisherman's attention.

Season, day and evening permits

*There are over 50 beautifully landscaped
reservoirs in the National Park, and
the larger ones offer opportunities for
angling, yachting and boating*

for boat or bank fishing from an
hour before sunrise to an hour after
sunset are available from the water
authority's offices in Bamford, *tel.*
(0433) 51424 and 51254. Day
permits are also available from the
offices in Matlock, *tel.* (0629)
55051; during licencing hours at
the Derwent Hotel in Bamford; the
Fisherman's Supplies at 131
Sheffield Road in Chesterfield – and
in the same town, the firm of
F Hall (Gunsmiths) Ltd, of
9 Beetwell Street.

Fees range from £3.60 for one
evening in a boat, to £130 for a
whole-season permit to fish
Ladybower. Various other options
are available in between.

CYCLE HIRE

Because some of the special trails
and paths laid out by the National
Park authority are along the track
beds of defunct railways they are
generally ideal for cycling, and it is
very easy for anyone who wants to
explore by bicycle – on the trails or
just round the charming Peak
District lanes – to hire a machine.

Ashbourne, see 'Tissington'
Edale Cycle Hire, open Easter
until October from the Rambler
Inn, Edale. *Tel.* (0433) 70268 or
(0332) 363929
Hartington Village Cycle Hire,
open from mid March to the end of
October. *Tel.* (029884) 459 or
(0335) 42629

Hayfield, see 'Sett Valley'
Lyme Park Cycle Hire, open from
late March. *Tel.* (06632) 2023
Middleton Top, see 'Tissington'
Monsal Head Cycle Hire, open all
year, except Christmas. *Tel.*
(062987) 505
Parsley Hay, see 'Tissington'
Sett Valley, for exploring the old
Hayfield to New Mills railway
route, open April until November.
Tel. (0629) 3411
Tissington and High Peak Trails,
for exploring two converted railway
trackbeds deep into the dales
country, open March until
November. Cycle-hire centres at
Ashbourne, Parsley Hay and
Middleton Top. *Tel.* (029884) 493
or (0629) 3411
Upper Derwent Valley, for
exploring the beautiful banks of the
Ladybower and Derwent
Reservoirs, open from March to
November. *Tel.* (029884) 493
Waterhouses Cycle Hire, scheme
based on the converted track of the
former Leek & Manifold Railway,
open from March to November.
Tel. (029884) 493

CRAFT WORKSHOPS

Old mills and other industrial
premises are being restored as living
museums in which modern
craftsmen exercise both traditional
and new skills.

*Most Blue John workings in the Peak
are exhausted, though small items
made of the mineral are still found in
many local craft shops*

Ashbourne
At *Derwent Crystal* in Shaw Croft
car park, visitors can watch full
English lead crystal being blown and
decorated by craftspersons. *Tel.*
(0335) 45219

Calver Bridge
The *Derbyshire Craft Centre* (2 miles
north of Baslow on the A623),
displays and offers for sale the best
of local and national craft products.
Refreshments are available, and
there is even a childrens' playroom.
Tel. (0433) 31231

The colourful spectacle of Market Day at Chapel-en-le-Frith

Chapel-en-le-Frith

Cameron Pearson is a small metal-working firm – a most appropriate pursuit in this ex-mining area – specialising in cast-aluminium, brass and bronze signs and plaques. Particularly popular are house nameplates decorated in relief. It is located near Stockport, close to the junction where the A6 meets the Sheffield road. *Tel. (0298) 2740*

Hartington

Close to the start of a Dovedale footpath, near the centre of Hartington village, is *Rooke's Pottery* – where original terracotta ware can be seen in production. Firsts and seconds in glazed and unglazed garden pots are available, and items for the home. *Tel. (029884) 650*

Longnor

Delightfully-named *Fox Country Furniture* makes just that – solid elm and oak items with clean and simple lines. Installed in The Old Cheese Factory at Reapsmoor (just 2 miles south of Longnor, on the B5053), the firm offers a wide range that includes most household requirements – and is always open to a challenge. *Tel. (029883) 496*

Actually in Longnor Market Place is the sculpture studio *Woodstringthistlefoss,* where visitors can watch artists working in porcelain, earthenware, stone, wood and metal. *Tel. (029883) 587*

Two Rivers Studio – at Mount Pleasant, Top o' th' Edge – specialises in spinning wheels and accessories made in ash and mahogany. Spinning demonstrations are also given, often on request. *Tel. (029883) 481*

Rudyard

Housed in the Old Post Office, Lake Road, is the *Daisybank Pottery* – a studio offering hand-thrown stoneware for both practical and ornamental use. *Tel. (053883) 656*

Tideswell

The Tideswell Dale Rock Shop, in Commercial Road, claims to be the only place in Derbyshire where Ashford black 'marble' is still used and worked in the traditional manner. Offered too are ornaments made of Blue John, also a local mineral. *Tel. (0298) 871606*

Waterhouses

In the *Staffordshire Peaks Arts Centre* (5 miles from Dovedale on the A52) is displayed a wide variety of paintings and craft products. Exhibitions and other events are regular features, and refreshments are available. *Tel. (05386) 431*

Youlgreave

Modern sterling silverware and jewellery is made on the premises at *Asquith Silver. Tel. (062986) 204*

GOLF

Ashbourne, at Clifton, *(1½ miles south-west on A515)* – 9-hole parkland course. *Tel. (0335) 42078*

Bakewell, off Station Road *(east side of town on the B6408)* – hilly 9-hole parkland course with plenty of natural hazards and magnificent views over the Wye Valley. *Tel. (062981) 3229*

Bamford, Sicklehome club, *(¾ mile south on A6013)* – 18-hole downland course with fine views. *Tel. (0443) 51306*

Buxton, Cavendish club, *(¾ mile west of town centre, off A53)* – 18-hole park and downland course under high hills and open to the west wind. *Tel. (0298) 3494*

Buxton and High Peak club, at Town End, Fairfield *(1 mile north east off A6)* – lovely 18-hole meadow course. *Tel. (0298) 3453*

Chapel-en-le-Frith, at The Cockyard, Manchester Road *(1 mile west on A6)* – fairly easy 18-hole course. *Tel. (0298) 812118*

Chesterfield, Stanedge club, Walton Hay Farm, Walton *(5 miles south west off B5057)* – hilly, moorland 9-hole course in exposed position. *Tel. (0246) 566156*

Tapton Park club, at Murray House, Tapton *(½ mile east of Chesterfield Station)* – 18-hole parkland course with some hard walking. *Tel. (0246) 566156*

Glossop, on Hurst Lane, off Sheffield Road *(1 mile east off A57)* – 11-hole moorland course in excellent position and with good natural hazards. *Tel. (04574) 3117*

Macclesfield, at The Hollins *(south-east side of town centre, off A523)* – hilly-heathland, 12-hole course on the edge of the Pennines. Excellent views. *Tel. (0625) 23227*

Matlock, on Chesterfield Road *(1 mile north east on A632)* – 18-hole moorland course with fine views. *Tel. (0629) 2191*

New Mills, at Shaw Marsh *(½ mile north, off B6101)* – 9-hole moorland course with wide views and first-class greens. *Tel. (0663) 43485*

Stocksbridge, on Royd Lane, Townend, Deepcar *(south side of town centre)* – hilly, 18-hole moor course. *Tel. (0742) 882003*

NATIONAL PARK INFORMATION CENTRES

The Peak District National Park is large and in places very isolated, but it is well serviced by special information centres that will supply visitors with accurate detail of all types – from topographical descriptions to the latest news on accommodation and car parking.

Bakewell

Run jointly with the West Derbyshire District Council, Bakewell Centre is open daily from 9.30am until 5.30pm, but closed on Thursdays during winter. *Tel. (062981) 3227*

Castleton

Open daily between Easter and the end of October from 10am to 6pm, and on winter weekends from 10am to 5pm, this centre stands in Castle Street near the parish church. *Tel. (0433) 20679*

Derbyshire Bridge – Goyt Valley

Open Sundays and Bank Holidays from Easter to September

Edale – Fieldhead Information Centre

Open daily from 9.00am to 5.30pm, this is situated on the right-hand side of the road which runs from Edale Railway Station to the village itself. *Tel. (0433) 70207*

Fairholmes – Derwent Valley

Open daily from Easter until the end of September, plus weekends only through October, from 10.30am to approximately 5.30pm

Hartington Old Signal Box

Open at weekends and on Bank Holiday Mondays from Easter to the end of September, 11am to approximately 5.30pm.

Mobile Information Centre

This caravan attends various outside events in the Peak during the summer months

Torside – Longdendale Valley

Open weekends and Bank Holidays, plus Mondays from Easter to the end of September – 11am to approximately 5.30pm

PLACES TO VISIT

Besides offering a wide and varied choice of landscapes to explore, the Peak District is rich in other places that amply repay a visit. Brief details of the best-known and most impressive follow, though it should be remembered that this list is by no means exhaustive.

Dates, times and similar details relating to such places have a tendency to change, so it is always a good idea to check with a local information centre before making a special trip – particularly to one of the big houses. Dogs are not welcome in many places open to the public even outdoor attractions, and certainly should not be let loose in park or farm land.

CAVES

Bradwell *Bagshawe Cavern*
This system of show caves is open from Easter to October. Visits can be made at other times by advance booking, and a special adventure trip is offered by appointment. *Tel.* (0433) 20540/21298

Castleton *Blue John Cavern and Mine*
Famous source of the Castleton mineral that gave it its name, the cave is open all year except Christmas Day, Boxing Day and New Year's Day. *Tel.* (0433) 20638

One of the great attractions of the Speedwell Cavern, near Castleton, is a half-mile underground canal along which visitors can travel by boat to investigate an old working face

Peak Cavern
Once the shelter for a rope-making village, this huge cavity in the rocks near Castleton is open between Easter and mid September. *Tel.* (0433) 20285

Speedwell Cavern
Open all year except on Christmas

Day, Boxing Day and New Year's Day. *Tel.* (0433) 20512

Treak Cliff Cavern and Mine
Open all year except on Christmas Day, this is a fine example of the combined natural and artificial excavations found near Castleton. Visitors can eat their packed lunches in an undercover area at the entrance, able to accommodate 250 people. *Tel.* (0433) 20571

HOUSES, PARKS & GARDENS

Alton Towers
Set near Alton in the former estate of the Earls of Shrewsbury, this huge leisure park and conference centre is renowned for its extravagant rides and shows. It is also famous for its beautiful gardens, which have been carefully restored round the ruins of the house. Open from Easter to the end of October. Refreshments. *Tel.* (0538) 702200

Buxton Pavilion Gardens
Gardens and woodland walks covering some 23 acres, around a pavilion erected in 1871 to a design by Milner, assistant to Joseph Paxton. An indoor swimming pool is filled with spa water, and there is a beautiful conservatory. Also of note are the Opera House, Concert Hall, Cafeteria and Lounge Restaurant. Grounds open all year. *Tel.* (0298) 3114

Chatsworth
This splendid home of the Dukes of Devonshire, 3½ miles east of Bakewell, has its own theatre and is beautifully sited in extensive grounds. Open from March to October. Closed sometimes for special events, for which bookings can be made. Guided tours are by prior arrangement, and refreshments are available.

Open from March until September is the Chatsworth Farm and Adventure Playground. There is no entry fee for access to Chatsworth Stand Wood Walks, though a stipulation is that children should be accompanied by an adult. *Tel.* (024688) 2204

Chestnut Centre
Just off the A625 between Chapel-en-le-Frith and Castleton, visitors can stroll through 40 acres of landscaped grounds and may be able to enjoy the rare privilege of watching otters playing in their natural surroundings. The centre is also a sanctuary for owls – for which there are special breeding enclosures – and falcons. Other features include an illustrated nature trail, picnic areas and refreshments. Open between April and October. Charge. *Tel.* (0298) 814099, (0625) 878980, or (0298) 812003

Ednaston Manor
At Ednaston, near Ashbourne, this Lutyens house stands in gardens of considerable botanical interest. Open weekdays, Easter until

September. Refreshments. *Tel.* (0335) 60325

Gulliver's Kingdom and Royal Cave
Theme park with over 40 rides and attractions at Matlock Bath, all covered by one initial entrance payment. Open daily from Good Friday until mid September. *Tel.* (0629) 55970

Haddon Hall
Two miles south-east of Bakewell, this delightful, medieval manor house is owned by the Dukes of Rutland. Open to the public from March to September, but not Mondays nor Sundays in July and August. Refreshments. *Tel.* (062981) 2855

Hare Hill
Four miles north-west of Macclesfield, this walled garden is owned by the National Trust. Set in parkland, it is known for its rhododendrons and azaleas. Open April until end October. Parties by written appointment. Dogs on leads

Heights of Abraham
Known mainly for the views which their situation affords over large areas of Derbyshire and its surrounding counties, these landscaped woodlands are perched high on southern slopes above Matlock Bath and may be reached by an exhilarating cable-car ride over the Derwent Valley. The best vantage point for an impressive panorama is Prospect Tower, which is of Victorian vintage. Both it and the grounds are open all year. An admission fee should be expected and there are mine tours available.

Kedleston Hall
Some 4 miles north west of Derby, this fine Adam mansion stands in a 500-acre park and has been the home of the Curzon family since 1100. Features include a magnificent marble hall, state rooms and a good collection of pictures. Lakes in the park support a colony of Canada geese. Also of interest is a 12th-century church, and a museum of the Indian culture. *Tel.* (0332) 842191

Lea Gardens
Three and a half acres of woodland, rock and alpine gardens, including a good showing of rhododendrons in June (4 miles south-east of Matlock, off the B6024). Open March to July, refreshments. *Tel.* (062984) 380

Lyme Hall and Park
Situated mainly west of Disley, part of the 1,321-acre tapestry of park, mixed woodland and moor that surrounds the great house on which this National Trust estate is centred has been designated a country park. Red deer descended from a herd that was here in Elizabethan times or earlier still roam free, and have

been joined by fallow deer. Appropriately, the rare small-leafed lime grows here, along with its more common cousin. The Cheshire Conservation Trust has a nature trail in the park, and there is an information centre in the hall. The grounds are open all year. Hall – March to September. *Tel.* (06632) 2023

Peveril Castle
Romantically situated above Castleton, this ruined Norman stronghold is looked after by English Heritage and open March to October. *Tel.* (0433) 20613

Poole's Cavern
Natural limestone cave in 100 acres of wooded country park, including a visitor centre with Roman exhibition and video show. Open Good Friday to November. Refreshments. *Tel.* (0298) 6978

Eagle owl, from Riber Castle

Riber Castle Fauna Reserve
Centred on a 19th-century castle ruin overlooking the River Derwent from the 853ft summit of Riber Hill is the last thing that anyone would associate with Derbyshire – a reserve in which colonies of European lynx live and breed in natural surroundings. It is not so surprising, however, when it is understood that this is a Rare Breeds Survival Trust Centre. Various types of sheep, pigs, cattle, goats, rabbits and poultry are kept there, as well as the cats. Open all year – except Christmas Day. *Tel.* (0629) 2073

MUSEUMS AND HERITAGE CENTRES

Bakewell *The Old House Museum*
This fine Tudor house off Church Lane is every bit as much of an exhibit as anything displayed in the folk museum which it contains. Particularly good features include open-timbered chambers and original wattle-and-daub interior walls. It is open from March until October, and at other times for parties by appointment. *Tel.* (062981) 3647

Biggin *Woodscroft Private Museum of Rural Life*
In the main street of Biggin, near Hartington, admission to this museum is free but by appointment only. *Tel.* (029884) 347

Buxton *Micrarium*
Claimed to be the first exhibition of its kind, a close look at nature through remote-controlled microscopes. In The Crescent. Open March until November. *Tel.* (0298) 78662

Museum and Art Gallery
History of the Peak District from its earliest geological past to its 'discovery' by tourists and romantics. Open all year, but not Mondays. *Tel.* (0298) 4658

Castleton *Cavendish House Museum*
Open daily all year except on Christmas Day, Boxing Day and New Year's Day. *Tel.* (0433) 20638/20642

Losehill Hall
This houses the Peak National Park Study Centre, near Castleton, where groups are welcome to illustrated talks about all aspects of the park and its activities. Farm visits, guided walks and refreshments are also available from the centre. *Tel.* (0433) 20373

Chesterfield *Peacock Information and Heritage Centre*
Historical displays in a medieval timber-framed building, in Low Pavement, that may have been a guildhall. Open weekdays. *Tel.* (0246) 207777/8

Eyam *Private Museum*
Local-interest exhibits giving an insight into the tragic but courageous past of this one-time plague village. Admission is by prior appointment only. *Tel.* (0433) 31010

Macclesfield *Heritage Centre*
Town history exhibition in a former 19th-century Sunday School, plus silk exhibition. Open all year.

Museum and Art Gallery
Contains a notable collection of Egyptian artefacts, plus work by artists Tunnicliffe and Landseer. In

The remains of Magpie Mine, near Bakewell, are among the best preserved of any lead workings in Britain

West Park, Prestbury Road. Free entry, open Easter until September. *Tel.* (0625) 24067

Matlock Bath *Aquarium*
Includes more than 40 aquaria, and a thermal pool where visitors may feed the fish. Open all year, weekends only in winter. *Tel.* (0629) 3624

Winster *Market House*
Stone-built, 16th and 17th-century market house in Winster's main street – contains a National Trust information centre. Open April to September, no charge.

Wirksworth *Heritage Centre*
Within Crown Yard – near the Market Place – are interpretive town-history displays, plus a working smithy, silversmith, cabinet maker and picture framer, all operating from a close, craft-oriented community. Open all year. *Tel.* (062982) 2210

STEAM, MILLS AND MINES

Bakewell *Magpie Mine*
Surface remains 3 miles west of Bakewell that are considered the best example of a 19th-century lead mine in Britain. Full information is available from the Peak District Mining Museum (Matlock). *Tel.* (062981) 3834

Buxton *Peak Rail*
Occasional steam rides from the Midland Railway site at Station Approach, Buxton. Site open all weekends. *Tel.* (0298) 79898

Cheadle *Foxfield Steam Railway*
Standard-gauge steam railway south-west of the National Park at Blythe Bridge, near Cheadle, including a museum of static displays. Open Easter until September. Refreshments. *Tel.* (0782) 314532

Cheddleton *North Staffordshire Steam Railway Centre*
About 4 miles south of Leek, this railway museum is housed in the Jacobean-style station. Open Easter to September. *Tel.* (0538) 360522

Flint Mill
By the Caldon Canal at Cheddleton are two old mills – one of 17th-century date for grinding corn (not working) and the famous flint mill. There is also a museum. Open at weekends. *Tel.* (078139) 2561

Crich *Tramway Museum*
Excellent use of an old limestone quarry in Matlock Road, Crich (off B5035). Vintage trams from all over the world on display. Rides and refreshments available. Open weekends and bank holidays, plus other times. *Tel.* (077385) 2565

Cromford *Arkwright's Mill*
The world's first water-powered cotton mill and associated buildings. Open all year. Refreshments.
Tel. (062982) 4297

Good Luck Lead Mine
Drift working near Cromford on the Via Gellia, being preserved to house an underground lead-mining museum. Open the first Sunday of the month, or at other times by arrangement. Adventure potholing-trips offered. *Tel.* (0246) 72375

High Peak Junction Workshops
In Lea Road, Cromford, these are the original workshops of the Cromford and High Peak Railway, now restored and containing an exhibition. Open weekends, and midweek during school and bank holidays. Refreshments.
Tel. (062982) 2831

Wharf Steam Museum
Collection of stationary steam engines, open when Leawood Pumphouse is not operating. Passenger horse-drawn boat services depart from here on summer afternoons. *Tel.* (062982) 3727

Glossop *Dinting Vale Railway Centre*
On the outskirts of Glossop, a collection of restored locomotives and other railwayana, open weekends and bank holidays from

March until October. Steam weekends at various times. Refreshments. *Tel.* (04574) 5596

Leek *Brindley Mill and Mill Museum*
Corn Mill designed by James Brindley in 1752, restored to working order and set in a delightful water garden in Mill Street. *Tel.* (0538) 384195

Macclesfield *Paradise Mill*
Working Victorian silk milk in Old Park Lane, with comprehensive supporting displays. Open afternoons all year except Mondays, Christmas and New Year. Refreshments. *Tel.* (0625) 618228

Matlock *Heights of Abraham*
Above the village of Matlock Bath in landscaped woodland are the easily-toured Nestus Mine and – for the more adventurous – the calcite and fluorspar deposits of Great Masson Cavern. One or all features open from Easter until October. Refreshments. *Tel.* (0629) 2365

High Tor Grounds
Roman lead workings and caves can be explored on High Tor, above Matlock, which also gives excellent views. Refreshments plus woodland walks, picnic areas and a playground for children. Open daily. *Tel.* (0629) 3289

Leawood Pump House
Beam engine of 1849 restored to working order by the Cromford Canal Society, off the A6 about 3 miles south of Matlock Bath. Open only by prior arrangement. *Tel.* (062982) 3727

Peak District Mining Museum
History of the Derbyshire lead-mining industry in all its aspects is interestingly displayed in this Matlock museum in The Pavilion, which also boasts the only 19th-century water-pressure pumping engine in Britain. Open February to mid October. *Tel.* (0629) 3834

Static and mobile exhibits from all over the world can be seen at the Tram Museum in Crich, while at Matlock Bath the Peak District Mining Museum gives an excellent history of local mineral exploitation

Temple Mine
Old lead and fluorspar workings off the A6 near Matlock, reconstructed as they were in the early 20th century. Open Easter until October. *Tel.* (0629) 3834

Middleton-by-Wirksworth
Middleton Top Engine House
Displays relating to the Cromford & High Peak Railway, and restored engines often in steam. Open Easter to November. *Tel.* (062982) 3204

Millers Dale *Limekilns*
Two sets of 19th-century industrial limekilns near Millers Dale Station, some 5 miles east of Buxton. Open all year.

Rowsley *Caudwell's Mill*
Visits to this historic working flour mill can be made by parties of 15 or more at most times, so long as prior arrangements have been made with the manager. Details of numerous public days, when visitors can tour the restored building, should be sought near the date of the proposed visit. *Tel.* (0629) 734374

WALKS AND TRAILS

The seasoned walker used to coping with the difficulties of rough country will almost certainly want to sample the wonders of off-road Peakland – but there is nothing to stop less experienced ramblers from enjoying the splendid scenery at first hand too.

In both town and countryside there are plenty of opportunities for joining guided walks led by rangers or other capable people, and the whole National Park is criss-crossed with trails that are often easy going because they have been laid out along the level track beds of defunct railways. Brief details of options that are available follow, and more information can be obtained from any National Park centre or by writing to The Peak National Park, Aldern House, Baslow Road, Bakewell, Derbyshire. *Tel.* (062981) 4321.

TOWN WALKS

Historical and architectural features of three main Peakland towns, Glossop, Castleton and Buxton, are brought to life on summer afternoons and evenings by information trails that last for about an hour and a half and start in all three cases from the local Tourist Information Centres. The Glossop one is on the railway-station forecourt, the one at Buxton on The Crescent and Castleton's near the church in Castle Street.

DISCOVERY TRAILS

Somewhat stiffer than the town walks, these offer the opportunity for individuals or families to explore the Peak in the company of experts in particular subjects. Telephone booking on Bakewell (062981) 4321 is essential – between 8.45am and 5pm Monday to Thursday, or up to 4.45pm on Friday – during the fortnight leading up to any trail. Also, it saves a lot of trouble if anyone who decides not to go after booking informs the organisers of that fact.

The leader will always be at the start of the walk at the appointed time, no matter what the weather, but the decision to proceed is his alone. Generally, the equipment required is limited to stout shoes, warm clothing and waterproofs, though the walkers are informed where specific items are needed for a particular trail.

Dogs are a danger to livestock and should be left at home, but children accompanied by adults are welcome. All-day trails can be expected to last four to six hours.

Full details of the Discovery Trails programme can be found in the National Park's free newspaper, *Peakland Post*, available from information centres.

RANGER RAMBLES

Ranger walks take place throughout the summer and last for up to six hours, starting at a number of venues named in a list that can be supplied by information-centre staff. Some make use of the Peak trails along old railway track beds, farm lanes, footpaths and field edges. Others follow less obvious courses. The three things they all have in common is that they are free of charge, limited to parties of 12 or less and are not suitable for children under 12.

Equipment can be limited to good footwear, warm clothing, waterproofs and a packed meal. If anything else is required the walkers will be informed before the event. Once again, dogs are not welcome due to the nuisance they can cause to stock animals.

High Peak Trail

Runs west then north west from Wirksworth, outside the south-eastern boundary of the National Park, and quickly climbs on to high ground – where it meets the Tissington Trail at Parsley Hay. Cycles can be hired at both Wirksworth and Parsley Hay.

Manifold Track

Runs north along the Manifold Valley and River from the A523 near Waterhouses – where there are cycle-hire facilities – at the southern edge of the National Park.

Monsal Trail

Perhaps the best known of all the National Park paths, follows the River Wye across the high heartland of the White Peak, running east to west from Bakewell to Buxton. Not only is it a beautiful walk in its own right, but the towns at either end are charming and interesting places to explore.

Pennine Way

The longest and most severe footpath in the country, starts by the 'Nag's Head' pub in beautiful Edale village. Immediately it climbs north to the high, peaty moorland of Kinder Scout – notorious for robbing compassless walkers of their sense of direction, then crosses the main A57 Sheffield-to-Glossop road at Snake Pass. From there it continues north and north west to the National Park boundary, crossing the aptly-named Bleaklow and dropping into reservoir-fringed Crowden before climbing into the desolate bogs of Black Hill. This path – which forges 250 miles through England's roughest country to the Scottish border – is romantic, beautiful and highly dangerous, taking its toll of careless people every year. All parts of it should be treated with the utmost respect – particularly the section in the Dark Peak. It is not for the casual or ill-equipped walker.

Sett Valley

Short walk (or cycle ride) which crosses west to east into the National Park from New Mills, following the trackbed of the former Hayfield to New Mills railway. Dominating the eastern skyline is the gritstone Dark Peak, with the great bulk of Kinder Scout prominent.

Tissington Trail

Runs generally north alongside Dovedale from Ashbourne, and climbs to join the High Peak Trail near Parsley Hay. Cycles can be hired at Ashbourne, just outside the southern boundary of the National Park, and at Parsley Hay.

Start of the Pennine Way (above), and walkers in the Ashopton Valley (left)

Calendar of Events

Although the items shown in this section usually happen in the months under which they appear, the actual times and dates of many vary from year to year. Also, there are other events such as fêtes, country shows, flower festivals, horse shows, demonstrations and the like which crop up regularly all over the National Park.

Haddon Hall, Chatsworth and similar centres are prime venues for such occasions.

In the case of uncertainty telephone the Peak National Park on (062981) 4321 – or call into any of its centres. Full and accurate information about what is going on from week to week is provided in the National Park's free newspaper, *Peakland Post*. The address for letters is Aldern House, Baslow Road, Bakewell, Derbyshire.

February
Winster Pancake Race, Shrove Tuesday
Ashbourne Ball Game, Shrove Tuesday & Ash Wednesday

April
High Peak & North East Cheshire Drag-Hunt point-to-point races, on Flagg Moor

May
Tissington Wells Dressing
Alstonefield Horse Show
Leek Arts Festivals
Endon Wells Dressing
Wirksworth Wells Dressing & Carnival
Middleton-by-Youlgreave Wells Dressing
Monyash Wells Dressing
Holmfirth Sing
Ashford-in-the-Water Wells Dressing
Bamford Sheepdog Trials
Castleton Garland Ceremony

June
Chelmorton Wells Dressing
Harden Moss Sheepdog Trials
Youlgreave Wells Dressing
Litton Wells Dressing
Tideswell Wells Dressing & Wakes Carnival
Hope Wells Dressing & Wakes
Winster Wakes Festivities
The Penistone Sing
Bakewell Wells Dressing & Carnival

Steam rallying is just one of many events held annually in the grounds of Chatsworth

July
Baslow Wells Week
Buxton Wells Dressing
Pilsley Wells Dressing and Fair
Buxton International Festival of Opera, Drama, Music & Dance
Stoney Middleton Wells Dressing

August
Bradwell Wells Dressing & Gala Week
James Brindley's Well Dressing, Wormhill
Macclesfield Forest Rush Bearing
Dovedale Sheepdog Trials, Ilam
Foolow Wells Dressing
Hope Sheepdog Trials and Agricultural Show
Lyme Championship Sheepdog Trials
Eyam Wells Dressing
Eyam Commemoration Service

September
Lognor Wells Dressing
Longshaw Sheepdog Trials
Wirksworth Clypping the Church
Longnor Wakes Gala
Chatsworth Horticultural Show
Hayfield Sheepdog Trials and Country Show
Hartington Wells Dressing

December
Hathersage Carol Singing

PEAK DISTRICT

Atlas

*The following pages contain a legend, key map and
atlas of the Peak District, three circular
motor tours and 16 planned walks.*

*Above: Winnats Pass, near Castleton. The road is closed to heavy traffic
and cars should negotiate it with care*

Peak District Legend

GRID REFERENCE SYSTEM

The map references used in this book are based on the Ordnance Survey National Grid, correct to within 1000 metres. They comprise two letters and four figures, and are preceded by the atlas page number.

Thus the reference for Buxton appears 91 SK 0673

91 is the atlas page number

SK identifies the major (100km) grid square concerned (see diag)

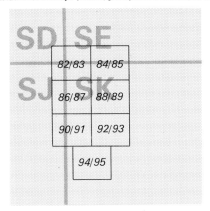

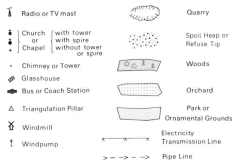

0673 locates the lower left-hand corner of the kilometre grid square in which Buxton appears

06 can be found along the bottom edge of the page, reading W to E

73 can be found along the right hand side of the page, reading S to N

TOURIST INFORMATION

Camp Site	Nature reserve
Caravan Site	Other tourist feature
Information Centre	Preserved railway
Parking Facilities	Racecourse
Viewpoint	Wildlife park
Picnic site	Museum
Golf course or links	Nature or forest trail
Castle	Ancient monument
Cave	Places of interest
Country park	Telephones : public or motoring organisations
Garden	PC Public Convenience
Historic house	▲ Youth Hostel

Mountain Rescue Post

◆ ◆ ◆ ◆ Waymarked Path / Long Distance Path / Recreational Path

ORIENTATION

True North At the centre of the area is 8'W of Grid North

Magnetic North At the centre of the area is about 6° W of Grid North in 1987 decreasing by about ½° in three years

ATLAS 1: 63,360 or 1" to 1 MILE

ROADS & PATHS Not necessarily rights of way

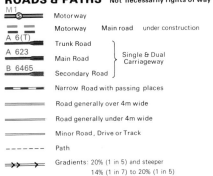

M1	Motorway
	Motorway Main road under construction
A 6(T)	Trunk Road
A 623	Main Road } Single & Dual Carriageway
B 6465	Secondary Road
	Narrow Road with passing places
	Road generally over 4m wide
	Road generally under 4m wide
	Minor Road, Drive or Track
	Path
	Gradients: 20% (1 in 5) and steeper 14% (1 in 7) to 20% (1 in 5)

GENERAL FEATURES

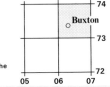

Radio or TV mast	Quarry
Church or Chapel {with tower, with spire, without tower or spire}	Spoil Heap or Refuse Tip
Chimney or Tower	Woods
Glasshouse	Orchard
Bus or Coach Station	Park or Ornamental Grounds
Triangulation Pillar	Electricity Transmission Line
Windmill	Pipe Line
Windpump	

RAILWAYS

Multiple or Single Track	Freight Line, Siding or Tramway
Narrow Gauge Track	Station (a) principal (b) closed to passengers
Bridges. Footbridge	Level crossing
Tunnel. Cutting	Viaduct. Embankment

WATER FEATURES

Marsh or salting, Towpath Lock, Aqueduct, Canal, Ford, Lake Weir Footbridge, Normal tidal limit Bridge, Canal (dry)

BOUNDARIES

National	County
National Park	District
NT National Trust	NT always open / NT opening restricted
FC Forestry Commission	Pedestrians only – observe local signs

ABBREVIATIONS

P	Post Office
PH	Public House
MP	Mile Post
MS	Mile Stone
LDP	Long Distance Path
CH	Club House
TH	Town Hall, Guildhall or equivalent
PC	Public Convenience (in rural areas)

ANTIQUITIES

VILLA Roman	Castle Non-Roman
Battlefield (with date)	
Tumulus	
Site of Antiquity	

PUBLIC RIGHTS OF WAY

Footpath	Road used as a Public Path
Bridleway	By-way open to all traffic

Public rights of way indicated by these symbols have been derived from Definitive Maps as amended by later enactments or instruments held by Ordnance Survey on 1st February 1986 and are shown subject to the limitations imposed by the scale of mapping. Later information may be obtained from the appropriate County Council.

The representation in this atlas of any other road track or path is no evidence of the existence of a right of way.

Danger Area   MOD Ranges in the area. Danger! Observe warning notices

HEIGHTS & ROCK FEATURES

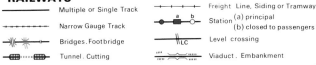

outcrop   cliff   scree

·144 Heights are to the nearest metre above mean sea level

Heights shown close to a triangulation pillar refer to the station height at ground level and not necessarily to the summit.

TOURS 1:250,000 or ¼" to 1 MILE

ROADS   Not necessarily rights of way

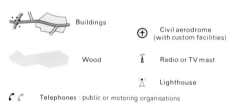

M 1 — Motorway with service area and junction with junction number

A 6(T) Dual Carriageway — Trunk road

A 623 Dual Carriageway — Main road

A 623 Dual Carriageway — Roundabout or multiple level junction

B 6106 Dual Carriageway — Secondary road

Other tarred road

Other minor road

Gradient 1 in 7 and steeper

RAILWAYS

Road crossing under or over standard gauge track

Level crossing

Station

Narrow gauge track

WATER FEATURES

Lake
Short ferry routes for vehicles
Bridge   Ferry
Canal
Transport for vehicles
Slopes
Cliff
Flat rock
Low water mark
High water mark
Dunes

ANTIQUITIES

Native fortress

Roman road (course of)

Castle • Other antiquities

CANOVIVM • Roman antiquity

GENERAL FEATURES

Buildings

Wood

Telephones : public or motoring organisations

Civil aerodrome (with custom facilities)

Radio or TV mast

Lighthouse

RELIEF

Feet	Metres	
		.274 Heights in feet above mean sea level
3000	914	
2000	610	
1400	427	
1000	305	Contours at 200 ft intervals
600	183	
200	61	
0	0	To convert feet to metres multiply by 0.3048

WALKS 1:25,000 or 2½" to 1 MILE

ROADS AND PATHS Not necessarily rights of way

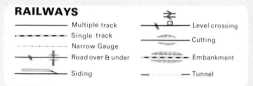

M 1	M 1	Motorway	............Path
A 64(T)	A 6(T)	Trunk road	Narrow roads with passing places are annotated
A 515	A 57	Main road	
B 6465	B 6105	Secondary road	
A 6(T)	A 57	Dual carriageway	

Road generally more than 4m wide

Road generally less than 4m wide

Permitted path and bridleway — Paths and bridleways along which landowners have permitted public use but which are not public rights of way. The agreement may be withdrawn.

Access Land   Access Land — Land open to the public by permission of the owner
Access Point

RAILWAYS

Multiple track
Single track
Narrow Gauge
Road over & under
Siding

Level crossing
Cutting
Embankment
Tunnel

GENERAL FEATURES

Church with tower
or with spire
Chapel without tower or spire

Gravel pit

Sand pit

Chalk pit, clay pit or quarry

Refuse or slag heap

Electricity transmission line
pylon pole

NT — National Trust always open

NT — National Trust opening restricted

FC — Forestry Commission pedestrians only (observe local signs)

National Park

HEIGHTS AND ROCK FEATURES

Contours are at 5 or 10 metres vertical interval

50 · Determined { ground survey
285 · by { air survey

Surface heights are to the nearest metre above mean sea level. Heights shown close to a triangulation pillar refer to the station height at ground level and not necessarily to the summit.

Vertical Face

75 60 50   100 70 50
Loose rock   Boulders   Outcrop   Scree

PUBLIC RIGHTS OF WAY

Public rights of way shown in this guide may not be evident on the ground

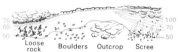

Public Paths { Footpath / Bridleway

++++++ By-way open to all traffic

Road used as a public path

Public rights of way indicated by these symbols have been derived from Definitive Maps as amended by later enactments or instruments held by Ordnance Survey between 1st Feb 1980 and 1st July 1983 and are shown subject to the limitations imposed by the scale of mapping.

Later information may be obtained from the appropriate County Council.

The representation on this map of any other road, track or path is no evidence of the existence of a right of way.

WALKS AND TOURS (All Scales)

7 — Start point of walk

→ Route of walk

Line of walk

Alternative route

3 — Start point of tour

→ Route of tour

Featured tour

Key to Atlas pages

Distances in miles to BUXTON
Map Ref: 91 SK 0673

Birmingham	66	London	158
Bradford	54	Manchester	24
Chester	70	Nottingham	56
Leeds	58	Sheffield	29
Liverpool	55	Stoke-on-Trent	22

PEAK DISTRICT

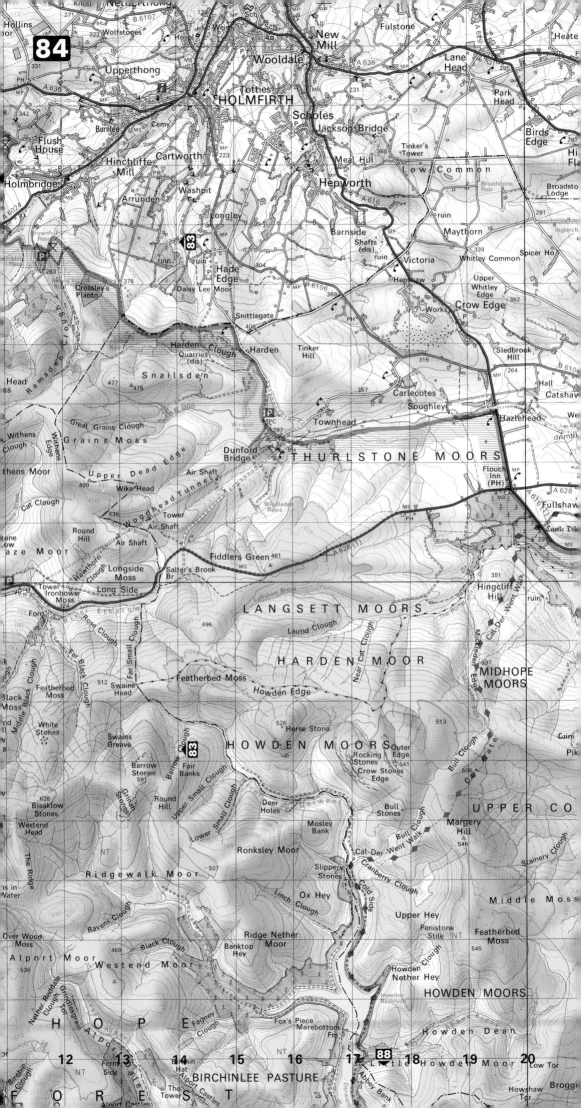

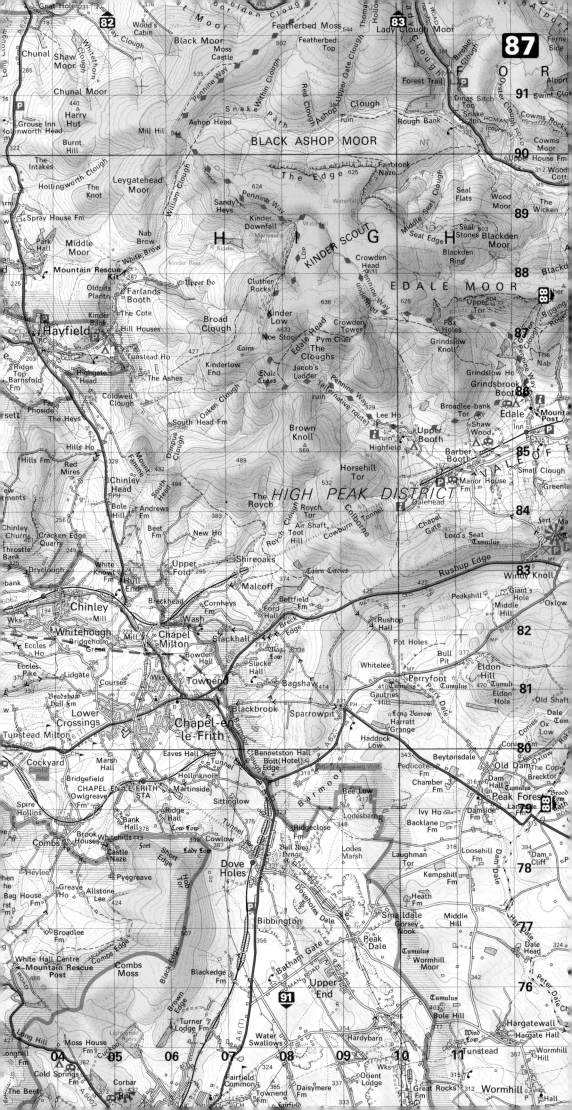

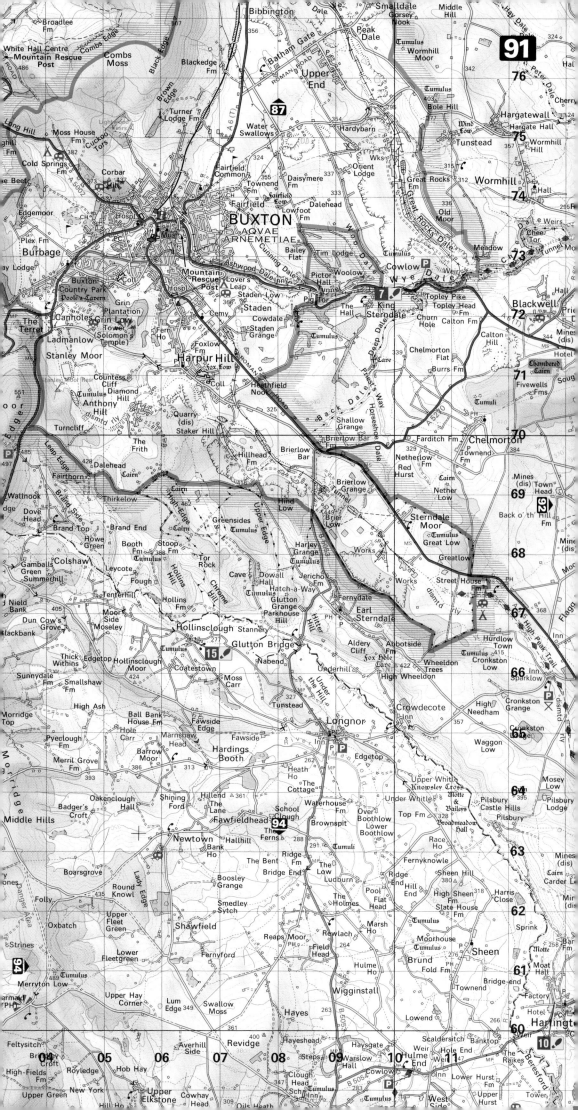

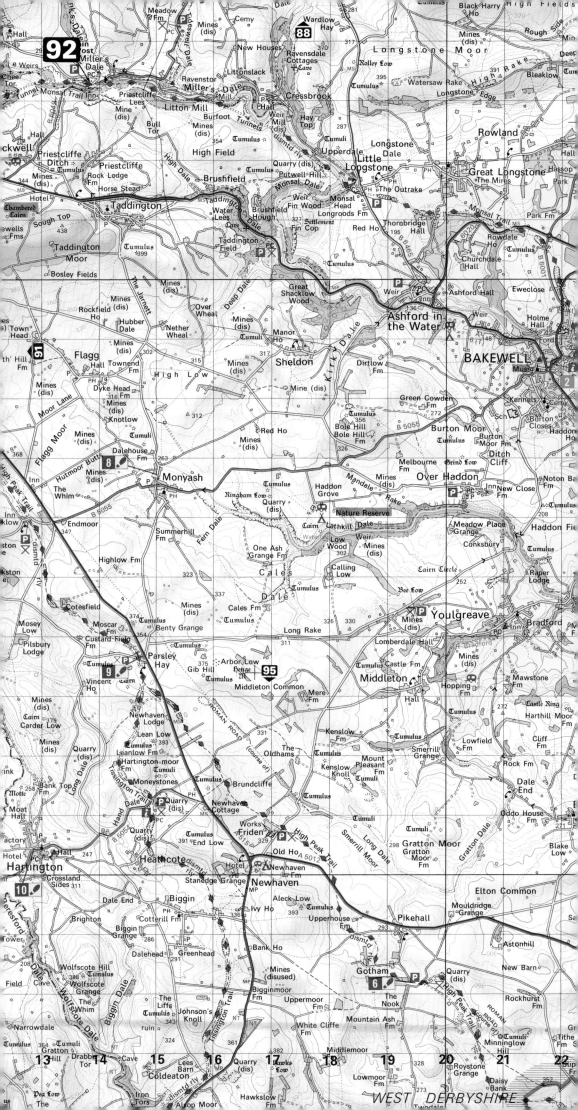

TOUR 1 51 MILES
Hills, Valleys and Caverns

The great scenic contrasts offered by the Peak District are appreciated on this drive. First is the dramatic transition from urban sprawl to a wild, open landscape. Then comes the chilly and mysterious darkness of caverns and mines beneath lofty hilltops soaring above village and valley. Probably the most dramatic of all is the distant view of the brooding Dark Peak, dominating the far end of Hope Valley.

The drive starts in the huge industrial city of Sheffield, *leaving along the A625 with Chapel-en-le-Frith signs, and climbing through the western suburbs before reaching open countryside after 4 miles. After 2 miles farther keep forward, signed Castleton, to remain on the A625. Enter the Peak District National Park, shortly crossing into Derbyshire, and after another mile reach the Surprise View.*

At this point along the A625 the whole of the Hope Valley suddenly opens up, with the 2,000ft ridge of the Dark Peak's Kinder Scout in the distance.

Descend into the Hope Valley and Hathersage (see page 50).

Memorial brasses to the Eyre family can be seen in Hathersage church, and the village has associations with Charlotte Brontë's *Jane Eyre*. A grave in the churchyard is traditionally held to be that of Little John.

Stay on the A625 to Hope (see page 51) and continue along the attractive valley to Castleton (Edale – see page 45 – may be explored as an addition to the main drive).

Castleton (see page 40) is as well known both on the ground and below it, for here are the famous caverns where the mineral Blue John was worked. The best known is the Blue John Mine, but the Speedwell and Treak Hill are also worth a visit. Peak Cavern is one of the area's most spectacular limestone caves.

Follow the main road through the village and in almost ½ mile turn left on to an unclassified road signed Speedwell Cavern.

North is Mam Tor – known as the Shivering Mountain because the limestone scree on its slopes is continually moving.

After a short distance pass the entrance to the Speedwell Cavern, then climb through the gorge of Winnats Pass and at the top turn right. In ¼ mile turn left to rejoin the A625 Chapel-en-le-Frith road. Alternatively, turn right to visit the Blue John Mine first. Continue west on the A625 beneath Mam Tor – passing a picnic site and an Edale turning on the right – towards Chapel-en-le-Frith.

In 1987 this small industrial and market town (see page 40), with its 17th-century market cross and old stocks, will be bypassed.

At Chapel turn left on to the A6 Buxton road, and in nearly 1½ miles turn left again on to the A623, signed Chesterfield. Continue to Sparrowpit and at The Wanted Inn, turn right, and later pass through the straggling village of Peak Forest. After 5 miles pass on the right the B6465 turn to Wardlow, then in ¾ mile turn left on to an unclassified road signed Foolow. Shortly turn left again to reach Foolow (see page 47). Turn right in the village and continue to Eyam (see page 46).

Now a commuter village, Foolow was once a lead-mining centre and is unusual in being built compactly round a village green – something of an oddity in the Peak. Eyam is famous for the great sacrifice made by its people in the 17th century, when plague came to the village.

At Eyam turn right on to the B6521, signed Bakewell, and enter wooded Middleton Dale. Reach a junction with the A623 and turn left, signed Chesterfield, and continue to Stoney Middleton.

The village (see page 63) is noted for its 18th-century octagonal church.

Continue to Calver (see page 39), and at the traffic lights turn left on to the B6001. Then turn right with the B6054, signed Sheffield via Frogatt Edge. Later cross the River Derwent, pass through attractive woodland and climb towards Totley Moor.

The ascent affords spectacular views left along the Hope Valley, with the Frogatt and Curbar Edges to the right.

Near the summit pass on the left the entrance to Longshaw (see page 54) Country Park (National Trust), then branch right, signed Dronfield. Continue across open moor to a junction with the A621, and at the gyratory system take the Sheffield road. Enter the southern fringe of the city, passing through the suburb of Abbeydale before reaching the city centre.

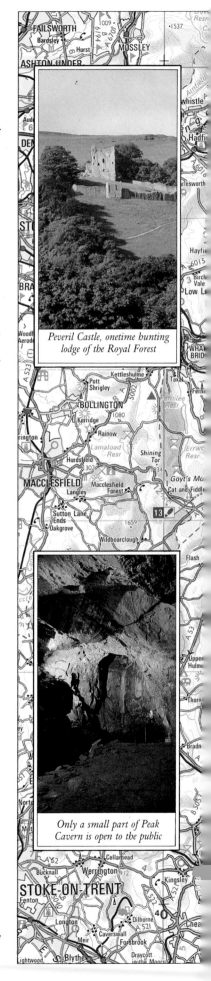

Peveril Castle, onetime hunting lodge of the Royal Forest

Only a small part of Peak Cavern is open to the public

Mam Tor, above Castleton, is now in the care of the National Trust. With the Winnats, it forms part of their 30,000-acre holding known as the High Peak Estate

TOUR 2 *40 MILES*
Mansions on the Wye

Unlike the open, windswept slopes and summits of the White Peak, many of its valleys are thickly wooded and a haven for wildlife. One in particular is the valley of the River Wye, whose irresistible combination of trees, clear water and weathered stone attracted the Dukes of Rutland and Devonshire to build great houses in its idyllic surroundings.

The drive starts from Bakewell (see page 35), a market town well known for the dessert sweet known as Bakewell Pudding – said to have been accidentally invented by a cook in The Rutland Arms during the 19th century.

Leave Bakewell on the A6, signed Matlock, and in nearly 2 miles reach the entrance to the mansion of Haddon Hall (see page 48).

Built by the Dukes of Rutland from the 12th to 17th century, this beautiful hall is everything that a medieval manor house should be. Its completeness is due to the fact that it was uninhabited for some 200 years and escaped the classical facelifts that were given to many old buildings.

Continue to Rowsley (see page 60), and after passing The Peacock Inn, turn left on to the B6012, signed Baslow. Pass the edge of Beeley (see page 37), cross the River Derwent and enter the attractive park of Chatsworth House (see page 41).

Known unofficially as The Palace of The Peak, Chatsworth is as complete an example of the neo-classical style as Haddon is of the medieval. Having the two so close together in the same lovely valley is a bonus, the like of which nowhere else in England enjoys.

Leave Chatsworth Park and continue to Baslow. Leave by the A623, signed Stockport and Manchester. Follow the Derwent valley to Calver (see page 39), meet traffic lights and turn left on to the B6001, signed Bakewell.

Baslow (see page 36) is an attractive little stone-built village grouped round a green, with a 17th-century bridge and tiny tollhouse.

Continue to Hassop, about 2 miles, and there branch right on to an unclassified road signed Great Longstone (see page 54). On reaching that village meet a T-junction and turn right, then continue through Little Longstone (see page 54) to reach the Monsal Head Hotel. Here turn right on to the B6465 Wardlow road, passing on the left a point which affords magnificent views of the great, horseshoe curve of Monsal Dale. Continue to Wardlow, and beyond that village turn left on to the A623, signed Stockport. In 1½ miles turn left again on to the B6049 and pass through the village of Tideswell (see page 64).

The splendid cruciform church in Tideswell, often referred to as The Cathedral of The Peak, was built relatively quickly between 1300 and 1370 – so, apart from the soaring Perpendicular tower, it is almost entirely in the Decorated style. The village itself is known for its wells-dressing ceremonies.

Stay on the Buxton road and in 1 mile pass on the left the Tideswell picnic area, then descend into Miller's Dale (see page 56). Pass beneath a railway viaduct and turn right on to an unclassified road signed Wormhill, then climb steeply with good views of Chee Dale to the left. Beyond the hamlet of Wormhill (see page 68) bear left, signed Peak Dale, and after a mile note on the left the extensive limestone workings of Great Rocks Dale. Continue with the Buxton road and descend, then climb and after a mile keep left. After another mile turn left on to the A6 for Buxton.

This attractive and park-filled spa resort wears its lineage on its sleeve, for though it was known to the Romans and early royalty its fine ranges of 18th- and 19th-century buildings leave no doubt as to when it achieved its greatest popularity.

Leave Buxton by the A6 Matlock road, following a winding course through the attractively-wooded gorge of the River Wye. Later, climb out of the valley to reach the outskirts of Taddington – at 1,139ft above sea level, one of the highest villages in England. After a short stretch of dual carriageway descend through wooded Taddington Dale, then 3 miles farther turn left on to an unclassified road signed Ashford village.

Sheepwash Bridge in Ashford on the Water (see page 33) is the oldest, narrowest and most picturesque of several that span the River Wye. Among the many mills here – mostly converted to other uses – is one where the decorative limestone known as Ashford Black Marble used to be cut and polished. The village dresses six wells in an annual ceremony.

Turn right through the village, and at the end turn right again, following Matlock signs. Re-cross the River Wye and turn left on to the A6 for the return to Bakewell.

The cascades in the gardens of Chatsworth

Bakewell Pudding – a cook's mistake at The Rutland Arms

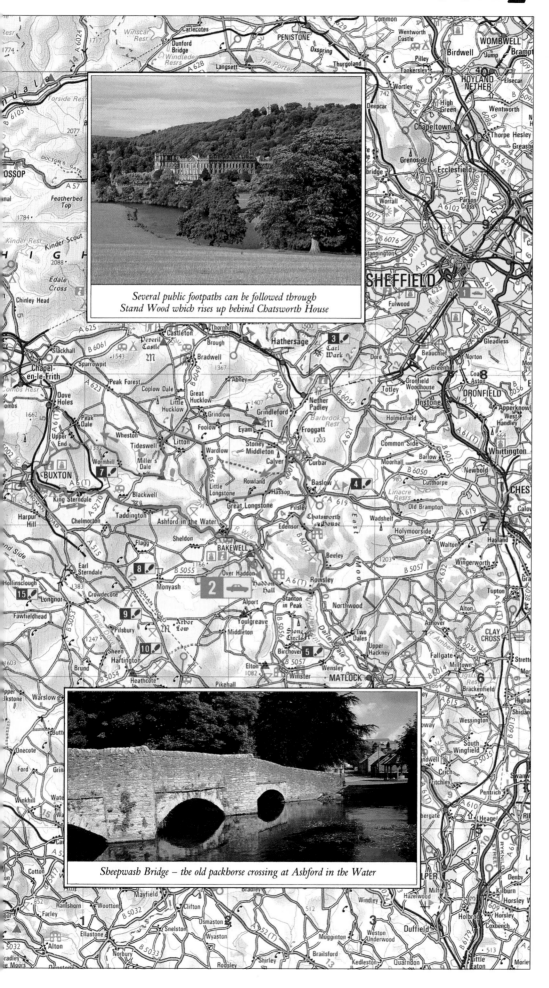

*Several public footpaths can be followed through
Stand Wood which rises up behind Chatsworth House*

Sheepwash Bridge – the old packhorse crossing at Ashford in the Water

TOUR 3 <small>51 MILES</small>
Peak Miniatures

As it winds through the south-eastern corner of the National Park this tour visits places of such diversity that it becomes an encapsulation of everything which is representative of the White Peak. Along the route are stone-built villages and rocky valleys, relics of early industry, grand houses set in wooded parkland and the spires of great churches built with the wealth from wool.

The drive starts in Matlock (see page 56) – the collective name for a loose gathering of individual settlements that were welded into a single spa resort in the 18th century.

From Matlock, follow signs Derby to leave the town by the A6, winding through a limestone gorge to the neighbouring spa village of Matlock Bath.

The impressive Heights of Abraham can be ascended by cable car. Of particular interest in the resort is the Peak District Mining Museum.

Continue along the A6 to Cromford (see page 43), and in the village turn right on to the A5012, signed Newhaven.

Cromford was where Arkwright built and operated the world's first water-powered cotton-spinning mill in 1771.

A short distance after leaving Cromford on the A5012 turn right for a long, winding climb through woodland on the Via Gellia valley road. After 4 miles reach crossroads and turn right on to the B5056, signed Bakewell. Continue across open countryside for 1¾ miles, then turn right on to an unclassified road signed Winster. Descend steeply into Winster (see page 68).

Leave Winster by the Bakewell Road, then ½ mile farther turn right and rejoin the B5056. Follow an undulating course for 2¾ miles, then cross a river bridge and turn right. Almost a mile farther on turn left on to the A6, signed Buxton, and shortly pass the car park for Haddon Hall.

This magnificent medieval manor house (see page 48) of the Dukes of Rutland dates from the 12th to 17th century and escaped neo-classical rebuilding.

Continue along the A6 to Bakewell (see page 35).

Bakewell is famous for the dessert sweet known as Bakewell Pudding, which can still be bought in the town.

Leave Bakewell by King Street, signed Monyash B5055.

In almost ¾ mile turn left on to an unclassified road signed Youlgreave. At the next T-junction turn right and continue over higher ground for 1¾ miles before descending a 1-in-5 slope to cross the River Lathkill. Beyond the bridge take the next turning left to reach Youlgreave (see page 69). At the church turn right (no sign), and in ¾ mile bear right signed Newhaven. After another ½ mile keep left, and in 2¾ miles pass on the left a turning into a picnic site. At the next T-junction turn right on to the A5012, then shortly turn left to join the A515, signed Ashbourne (see page 32), and pass the Newhaven Hotel. After 6 miles at crossroads turn left on to an unclassified road signed Tissington. Drive through parkland to Tissington (see page 66).

Return through the parkland, then turn left on to the A515 Ashbourne road and continue to Fenney Bentley (see page 66). Continue past the village for ½ mile, then turn left on to the B5056, signed Bakewell. After 2¾ miles turn right on to an unclassified road signed Bradbourne. At the post office in that secluded village turn right signed Carsington, and follow a pleasant byroad – narrow in places – for about 1¼ miles, then turn left on to the B5035 Wirksworth road. After another 1¼ miles drive alongside the northern extremity of the new Carsington Reservoir. Stay on the B5035 for a further 1¼ miles, then turn right signed Wirksworth (unclassified; light traffic only). Descend; (see page 68).

In the town centre turn left, then immediately right, with the B5035, signed Crich. Ascend on to higher ground, then follow a long descent into the Derwent Valley with views across to Crich Stand. At the foot of the descent turn right on to the A6, then cross the River Derwent and immediately go forward with the B3035 – still signed Crich. At the village cross turn left (unclassified) and follow signs to the Crich (see page 42) Tramway Museum.

On 940ft Crich Stand is a tower with a light, raised as a memorial to the Sherwood Foresters. The tram museum is sited in an old limestone quarry.

Continue with the unclassified road to Holloway and turn right into Church Street, signed Riber. In ¾ mile go over crossroads into Riber Road. Follow that byroad for 1½ miles, meet a T-junction and turn left, then ¼ mile later keep left and pass on the right the turning to Riber Castle Wildlife Park (see page 73). Descend steeply through hairpin bends, and at the foot of the slope turn right. Later turn left on to the A615 for Matlock.

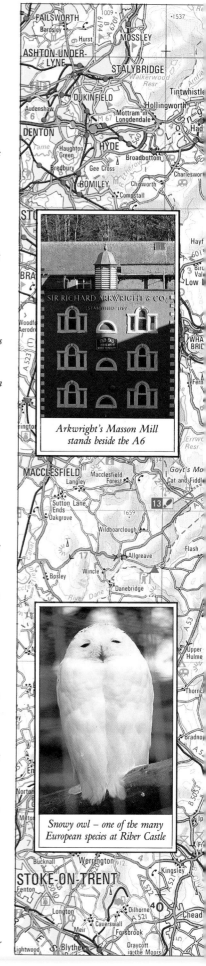

Arkwright's Masson Mill stands beside the A6

Snowy owl – one of the many European species at Riber Castle

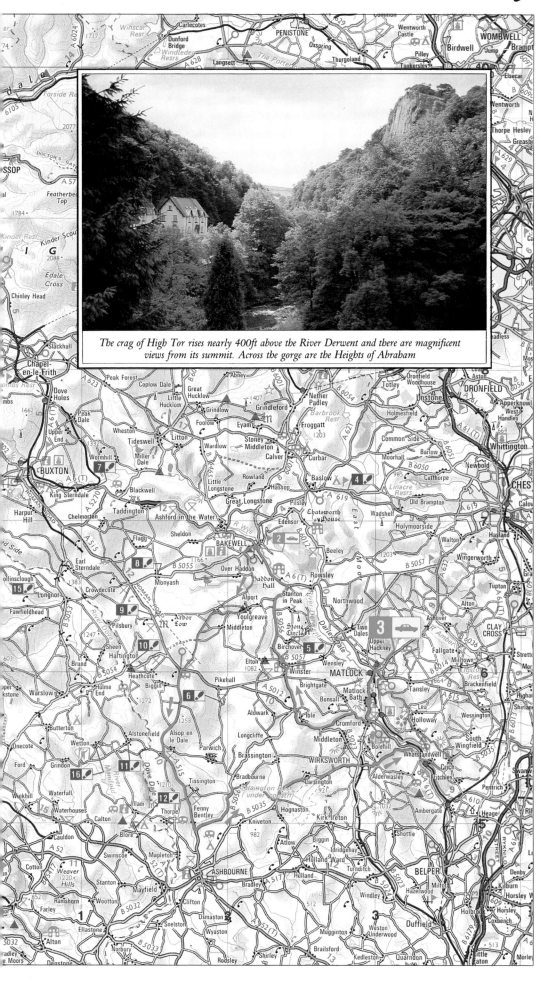

The crag of High Tor rises nearly 400ft above the River Derwent and there are magnificent views from its summit. Across the gorge are the Heights of Abraham

WALK 1
Woodlands by
Watersides

Allow 1½ hours

Unusual among Peak rambles in that it explores landscapes where woods and water predominate, this walk is free of hazard but affords splendid views of plantations and reservoirs from high ridgetop vantage points. At Fairholmes car park, where the walk starts, are an information centre, a picnic site and facilities for cycle hire.

Green woodpecker, also known as yaffle, or rain bird

Leave the car park (SK173893) along a tarmac road above the reservoir picnic area. Cross the main approach road, adjacent to Locker Brook, and follow a signpost direction up into the Forest Walk on a concessionary footpath. Reach a 'leat' – which captures water from Upper Locker Brook for the Derwent Reservoir – and cross this by means of a stile and footbridge. Continue ahead along a zig-zag path, with larch-stake steps at the steeper parts, keeping right at the junction with an exclusive path for the Lockerbrook Centre. Continue through a broken wall and turn left to leave the plantation by a stile. Follow waymarks up to a crosstrack junction. A right turn here leads to the shores of the Derwent Reservoir, at the foot of Ouzelden, but the walk continues left. Lockerbrook Youth Adventure Centre enjoys fabulous views of Derwent Dale.

After turning left at the crosstrack, go through a gate and climb to another crosstrack junction at the ridgetop. Go left here and walk along the edge of the Open Hagg Plantation. This part of the walk affords views into the Woodlands Valley, a 'hidden' place dominated by the shadowy northern edges of Kinder Scout, from Crookstone Knoll to Fairbrook Naze.

Continue along the high grass path to a stile and gate, where there is bridleway signpost indicating Glossop and Derwent. The waysign is a relic from a time before the village of Derwent was drowned,

when this path was a regular horse-riders' route between that isolated community and the outside world upon which it depended.

Descend the bridleway into a plantation and emerge from the trees at a gate. Continue down the 'Old Road' track and descend to the reservoir road beside Bridge End car park. Ahead on the skyline of Derwent Edge are the Wheel Stones – sometimes known as the Coach and Horses, due to their likeness in profile to a coach in mad flight across the moor. Before the creation of the Ladybower Dam in the mid 1940s the old road crossed the River Derwent at Bridge End – hence the name – close to Derwent Hall, which has also been lost.

Go left and branch right along a concessionary path leading through the woodland fringe between the reservoir and the road. During late spring or early summer this section of the route is carpeted with bluebells. Farther along is a rather ugly pipeline which relays water from the Derwent Dam to the Ladybower Treatment works.

From the pipeline, angle gradually up to the Derwent Overlook car park, then continue on a path alongside the road, slanting right and returning to the Fairholmes car park.

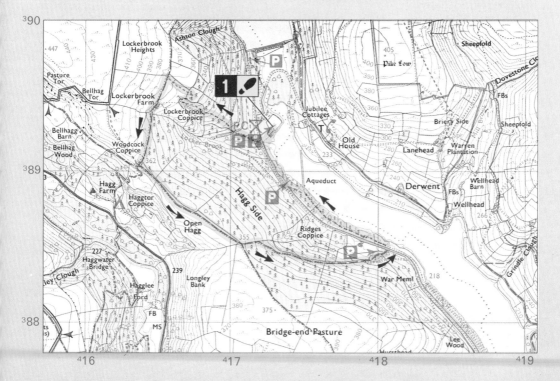

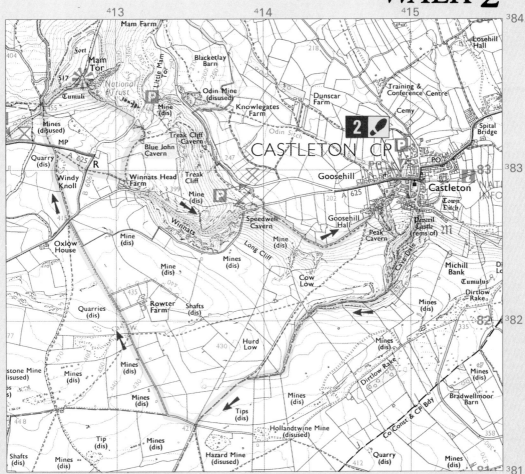

Caverns and a Castle Crag

Allow 2½ hours

Castleton is a Peakland resort of the best kind – offering plenty of scenic variety, both on the grand landscape scale and hidden underground in 'show' caves. Many fascinating geophysical secrets are revealed by close study of limestone bluffs that are effectively great fossil reefs, and echoes of distant man-made history are heard at ruined Peveril Castle. It should be remembered that the time estimate for this walk does not consider visits to places of interest.

Starting from the entrance of Castleton's main car park (SK149830), go left into the village and turn right into Castle Street – where there is an information centre. Ahead on its impressive natural bastion is ruined Peveril Castle, begun in 1176 by Henry II – possible on an Iron Age site. William de Peveril acted for Henry as forest bailiff.

Go left across the Market Square to the unobtrusive entrance of Cave Dale, which is to the right off Bargate. It is extraordinary that so large a dale should end in so narrow a passage, and farther into its rock-girt cleft it constricts yet again. Here, where a band of tough basalt lava once intruded into the original seabed limestones, a small stream makes a brief appearance before sinking through the dale floor into Roger's Rain House – in Peak Cavern.

The walk route continues along the dale, accompanied by these and other features, with the cleft gradually opening out and progress through boundaries facilitated by metal gates. Reach and cross a large pasture – passing a mere – and enter a small passage lane (note the sheep pens) to join Dirtlow Rake Lane. Turn right here, continue to where the lane widens and take the right-hand track. This is known as Rowter Lane. All this upland from Bradwell to Eldon Hill is streaked with lead veins which have been exploited since at least Roman times. Most recently many of the spoil heaps have been re-worked for fluorspar.

Continue beyond the Rowter Farm access on to a metalled surface, reach a cattle grid and cross the B6061 to climb Windy Knoll before descending to the right. Notable aspects of the limestone outcrop here include natural deposits of bitumen and the Bone Cave, where excavations by Victorians uncovered the bones of bison, brown bear, reindeer and wolf. A short, stiff climb from Windy Knoll is the scree-girt summit of Mam Tor, but care is required. A stepped path which descends alongside the slippery scree to the Blue John Mine and Treak Cliff Cavern makes an interesting addition or alternative to the walk.

This and the main walk meet at Winnats Head Farm. A minor road descends Winnats Pass (not suitable for heavy traffic) from here to the Speedwell Mine – noted for its underground canal.

At Winnats go through a gate and keep right, following a track through further gates to reach Goosehill Bridge, in Castleton. Anyone who missed the previous show caves should visit Peak Cavern, which is reached from the bridge along a narrow path running to the right.

To conclude the round trip, cross the bridge and follow the path downstream alongside Peakshole Water.

WALK 3

Stonechats, seen as pairs all year round

Millstone Grit Landscapes

Allow 1½ hours

Travellers approaching Hathersage on the A625 from Fox House Inn for the first time never fail to be surprised by the sudden Derwent Dale panorama that greets them when they burst through a breach in the high Millstone Edge. This scenic thrill is enhanced for the walker who climbs to Over Owler Tor across country that is unlikely to be boggy, but has heather and boulders that can trip the unwary and demands the protection of stout shoes.

Starting from the Surprise View car park (SK253802), cross a fence stile and climb a clear path through light birch woodland and gritstone boulders on to the Owler Tor edge. Continue through heather amongst gritstone blocks. Owler derives from 'alder tree'. Among the strange and varied gritstone

shapes all around can be found millstones that were cut on site and abandoned. The Millstone Grit from which they were fashioned is a coarse sandstone that forms the great edge which is crossed on the approach to Surprise View from Hathersage. In ancient times the stone was used for making corn-grinding querns, and more recently both this edge and nearby Lawrence Field were major sources of millstones. Many hundreds lie cut and forlorn in the woods below Surprise View.

Continue, noting the 'Smiling Tortoise' rock formation on the way to Mother Cap. There are many natural stone formations to enjoy along the way. Mother Cap is a giant stack which – like the summit rocks of Over Owler Tor – survived the gruelling attentions of the Ice Age. Its name has obvious parallels with Mam Tor (visited in Walk 2), since both mean 'Mother Hill' and in both cases they are associated with the sites of ancient settlements. When visibility is good Over Owler Tor is a superb viewpoint from which can be appreciated the deep cut of Derwent Dale.

Holding to the ridgetop through heather the walk eventually arrives at the gap of Winyards Kick, where the ridge is breached by an old hollow way that was used as a packhorse route. Identify a narrow but visible path to the right and descend it through heather, joining a more pronounced path just before a stream. Continue over close-cropped turf, dropping down to the A625 by the Toad's Mouth Rock. Go left, staying particularly vigilant for traffic while negotiating the sharp bend, and cross the road to a kissing gate signposted 'Padley via Padley Gorge'. Cross small cascades to a footbridge and follow the Burbage Brook downstream.

This section is popular with picnickers and paddling children – though the latter have nothing to do with the name of the gorge!

The next right turn is marked by a simple plank footbridge, after which the walk climbs a deeply-grooved packhorse route – known as the Hollow Gate – and returns to the start.

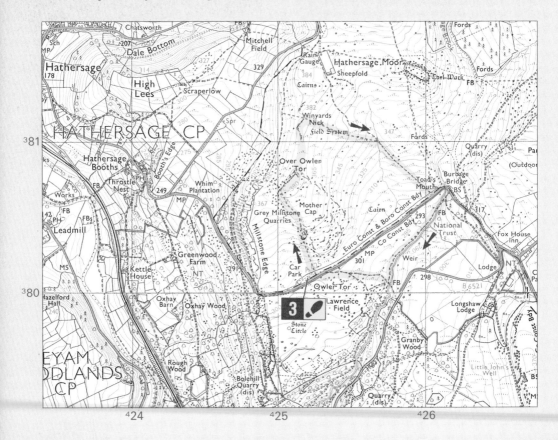

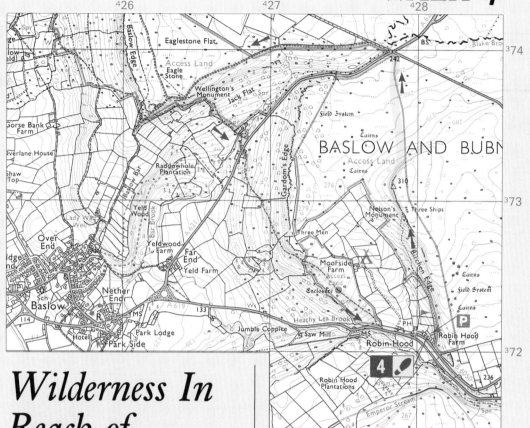

Wilderness In Reach of Chesterfield

Allow 2½ hours

West from the conurbations of Sheffield and Chesterfield rises a moorland slope that in its lower regions has been tamed, but which eventually soars to a broken skyline of wild crags forming the frontier bulwark of gritstone country. Not only is this impressive feature very beautiful, but – particularly in this century – it provides abundant recreational opportunities to visitors from town and country alike.

Wheatear, a summer visitor from Africa

From the Birchen Edge car park (SK281722) – just above the Robin Hood Inn – follow the B6050 left to a style on the left, signposted 'Birchen Edge'. Follow a clear path from the stile, through birchwood and boulders, to an outcrop beneath Nelson's Monument. Climb to the crest of Birchen Edge. Close to the monument, which was erected in 1810 by John Brightman of Baslow, are three isolated boulders on which have been incised the names *Royal Soverin (sic), Reliance* and *Victory*. Known collectively as the Three Ships, they commemorate Nelson's successes at the Battles of the Nile and Trafalgar. There are several easy lines of ascent to the edge, but also huge slabs of rock popular with climbers.

Follow the edge north, joining beyond the 1,017ft OS trig pillar an evident path. Descend along this, sometimes over wet moorland and along the boundary of access land, to a ladder stile. Cross this on to a minor road and go left. Cross the A621 at crossroads and climb past the infant Bar Brook to a gate on the left, from which continue along a track known as the Chesterfield Road. An interesting relic of bygone

days along this old way is a stone marker, or stoop, which dates from when the track was the main horse road between Chesterfield and Baslow. Also of interest is a 10ft-high obelisk raised in 1816 to the Duke of Wellington by E M Wrench '. . . late 34th Regiment'. Some 200yds north west of the monument is the Eagle Stone, the name of which is a corruption of 'eccles' and may signify that the spot was used for early Christian gatherings.

As the track descends it becomes rougher near an old quarry at the end of Baslow Edge. Here veer sharp left and follow the wall round and down to a narrow passage, via stiles, and to an old packhorse footbridge over Bar Brook. Cross and climb to the A621. Cross the road and round Cupola Cottage via two stiles, thereafter ascending a clear path beneath Gardom's Edge. At the third gap in the wall a diversion can be made to the left, climbing to the Three Men of Gardom viewpoint. The 'men' are ancient cairns.

The main route continues over the shoulder of the hill, crossing a Bronze Age ring enclosure to bring the walk back to the A619 Chesterfield road at a stile. Turn left here for the return to the car park.

0	200	400	600	800	1		2		3	Kilometres

0	200	400	600	800	1000		1			2 Miles

SCALE 1:25 000

WALK 5
Prehistory on Stanton Moor

Allow 2 hours

Moorland walks always exert a particular fascination, but when the moor is remote and rich in the relics of prehistoric peoples its air of mystery becomes intensified. That is certainly the case on Stanton Moor, an isolated gritstone 'island' known for its quality building stone and respected in the Bronze Age as a magical place. Here it is possible to wander among mounds, ringworks and stone circles that are the very stuff of prehistory.

Suitable car parking is found opposite the west entrance to Ann Twyford's Birchover Quarry (SK241624), on the Stanton in Peak to Birchover road. Facing the quarry entrance, turn left and walk along the road for about 400yds towards Stanton in Peak, then cross the road to the old New Park Quarry access track, between the posts of which is a large boulder. Follow the track to a stile and gate, cross, and ascend to the Cork Stone. Continue to the next track junction and turn left. Victorian whim gave metal handles to the blade-like Cork Stone. Just to the right of the subsequent track junction is a burial mound of which the size and form are still evident despite the ravages of time and clumsy excavation. In its central cist were found cremation remains of a dozen interments, with attendant food vessels and personal tokens.

Continue north (left) along the track, flanked each side by heather moor. Along this stretch of the walk are to be seen several Bronze Age features, including a sizeable ringwork to the left, just before

a birchwood. In an enchanted setting within the wood is the Nine Ladies stone circle, from which a great tumulus once rose. Until 1985 this and the associated King Stone were straitjacketed within walls – shown as a ring on OS maps.

In about 50yds turn right and follow a track to a fence stile. Cross this on to a path passing beneath the Reform Tower. The tower, for which there is no public access, was erected by the Thornhills of Stanton Hall in tribute to Earl Grey – who carried the Reform Bill through Parliament in 1832. Farther on the edge path meets the Cat Stone, which crudely resembles a feline profile.

After the Cat Stone continue on the edge path to leave this spur and forge south, with views to the left over Darely Dale and the ugly fluorspar works around the former Millclose Mine. Follow close to a fence – passing deep (and dangerous), heather-covered quarry workings – to reach a minor road. At the road turn right, and at the next road junction either turn right again to the starting point or turn left and descend Birchover village street to The Druid pub. In trees behind this romantically-named pub are Rowtor Rocks, which are well worth a visit.

The return from there is by a path which dips down and then climbs east between Dungeon Plantation up on the left and old quarries down to the right.

Mountain hare, smaller then the brown hare

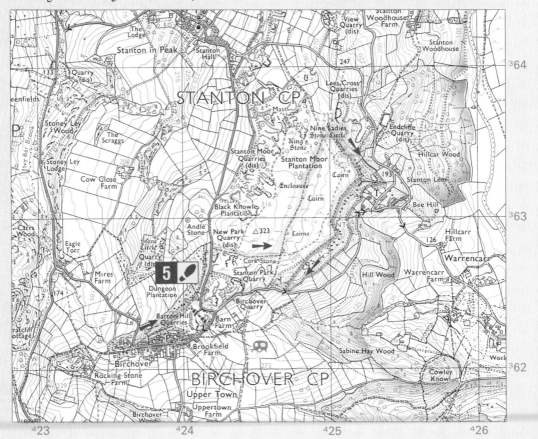

Relics of Old Industries

Allow 2½ hours

The landscapes of the Peak have a long and colourful tale to tell of peoples who from ancient times have arrived to carve out farms and delve deep in search of valuable minerals – then vanish, leaving only hill names, ruins and half-recognisable bumps in the ground as mute memorials to their efforts.

The walk starts in Minninglow car park (SK195582), near Pikeball and by a railway bridge over which the Cromford and High Peak line once ran. Begin by walking to the farthest end of the car park from the entrance and following 'Royston Grange Trail' signposts along the old track bed. As a railway venture the line can never have been a storming success, but its current use for recreational walking and cycling is quite the opposite.

Follow the trackbed round towards a large stone railway embankment below the bump of Minninglow Hill, passing quarry workings on the left and Minninglow Grange beside its mere in the valley to the right. Numerous quarries developed along the course of the railway, plus workings to extract high-firing silica sand, and refractory brickworks in which it was used. Minninglow Hill is crowned by a New Stone Age burial mound. Just after the hill on the left of the track bed is the stone beehive shape of an old lime kiln.

After the lime kiln meet a gate bearing a yellow waymark superimposed by a black 'R', blocking the track bed next to a National Park signpost. Cross this and note on the left another gate, also with a yellow mark bearing a black 'R'. This is the way the walk continues (the inviting gate and track diagonally opposite on the right should be ignored). Turn left to cross the waymarked gate and a wall stile into an old droving track known as Gallowlow Lane. Ascend past two fields on the right, and at the third keep a sharp lookout for waymarks directing the route back down the pastured slope to the trackbed, beneath which it passes by way of the Trail Bridge. On emerging from the Trail Bridge continue downhill through pasture to an end wall near the field's bottom-left corner. Cross this by a stile and follow the wall on the left through fields and over stiles to a farm track. Keep a careful watch all the time for waymarks. A left turn along the track leads to remains of the present 18th-century grange's 14th-century predecessor, which was owned by a Cistercian Abbey. Close by are remains of a pneumatic quarry pumphouse.

The main route is continued by turning right at the point where the cross-country path meets the farm track, and runs through the farmyard of the present Roystone Grange along a path that can be messy in bad weather.

Pass through gates and meet an improved section of track after Roystone Cottages, then meet a junction with Minninglow Lane and turn left. Continue to Cobblersnook crossways, where a choice of routes may be made. By turning right alongside Cobblersnook Plantation (left) the metalled lane may be followed back to the railway bridge and car park.

A longer alternative is straight ahead at the crossways to follow Cobblersnook Lane past The Nook cottage and up on to Upper Moor. In just under ½ mile keep right at a fork in the lane and later continue straight on to follow the boundary of an open field up the last rise and rejoin the lane at the intersection of two ancient packhorse ways. Turn right at this junction and follow Green Lane down a dry valley to rejoin the High Peak Trail after less than a mile. The walk is concluded by following the trackbed to the right round the tight sweep of Gotham Curve – above the hamlet of Pikeball – and back to the start. In its day the Gotham Curve which turns through 80 degrees, was the tightest of any British Rail line. Only short wheel-based locomotives and rolling stock could use it.

Gorges and the River Wye

Allow up to 3 hours

Beautiful as it is, this memorable walk amongst woodlands, rock and tumbling water cannot be recommended to everybody. One section in particular – at water level in the bottom of a gorge – includes stepping-stone ways through the river, rock-step clambers that can be very greasy in wet weather and a bankside that is ready to turn into mud at the least suggestion of rain. However, the first part along railway trackbeds is easy, safe walking.

The walk makes an unpromising start in Wye Dale car park (SK103724), on the A6 opposite the devastation of Topley Pike Quarry, but improves immediately along a riverside track running downstream through woods. Just before the third viaduct, climb steps in the bank to the right on to trackbed forming part of the Monsal Trail. At the top of the steps turn right. Pass through a cutting and alongside high crags, then cross the Wye and pass on the left a point where the main line once entered. Continue through two short tunnels to the sealed Chee Tor Tunnel, under Chee Tor. This section, as far as Chee Tor Tunnel, is flat, safe walking. After the first portal-like cutting is the dramatic peak of Plum Buttress on the right, which shows to particular advantage its wavy bedding planes of limestone. At the river crossing the Wye flows in a deep, wooded gorge rich in plants and animals.
However, it is suggested that young or infirm visitors turn back at the second short tunnel.
Before reaching the sealed entrance to Chee Tor Tunnel, leave the track bed along a permissive path to

the right and cross a footbridge just before passing beneath a railway bridge. Descend to the water's edge, and continue through a bankless defile by means of 44 stones set in the water below overhanging limestone cliffs. Continue – with care in wet weather – and after negotiating rough rock 'steps' above the river cross two small footbridges to skirt Wormhill Springs. After the track bed the path tunnels deep into the greenery of the gorge itself, with cliffs and crags looming both sides of a cut not much wider than the riverbed. Wormhill Springs is an extraordinary area where water gushes from a dozen places in the ground – with some force – and flows cold and clear across the ground into the river.

After another rock step (take care) continue to a waymarked footbridge and cross it. Climb directly up the slope opposite until about halfway, then veer slightly right, continuing the ascent to a stone wall. Cross this and the following one at stiles, then continue alongside a wall to the right. Follow the wall as it turns right and join a gated lane leading through Blackwell Hall farmyard. The pasture that is climbed from the river to the first wall features small stone enclosures that were built by the Celts. Views of Chee Dale from the top of the stiff climb are rewarding.

Past the farmyard meet a junction and bear round right with the metalled lane, eventually passing a farm shop and camping site on the right. Just after the site reach the gated entrance of a green lane on a left, 90-degree bend in the surfaced road. Follow the green lane between walls to its end, then continue along a track to a stile by a ruined barn. Cross this and head for a wall stile in the bottom-left corner of the pasture. Continue along the foot of the next field to another stile leading to rough ground a few paces from the dizzying precipice of Plum Buttress.
Instead of crossing the stile above the precipice, slant left on a path which descends steeply to a wall stile in a tiny valley which joins the main path. Descend right to the main valley floor and cross a stile next to the old railway bridge to rejoin the trail. From here retrace steps upstream to the Wye Dale car park.

SCALE 1:25 000

Lathkill Dale

Allow at least 3 hours

All the limestone dales of the White Peak's central plateau contain precious wildlife habitats, but perhaps the most notable is Lathkill – much of which is set aside as a National Nature Reserve. Visitors are on trust to enjoy this unique countryside without damaging or disturbing it, taking with them only memories and photographs when they leave.

This walk starts in Monyash from a National Park car-parking area (SK150667), and heads north along Chapel Street. When the road descends to a fork go right, then turn right again to enter Bagshaw Dale through a gate. Continue along the valley floor via stiles and gates to reach the B5055 Bakewell road. Cross this to a gate signposted 'Lathkill Dale' and enter the shallow upper dale. At a second stile the dale narrows, marking the beginning of the nature reserve. Continue through the twisting defile. A brief inspection of spoil from the disused Ricklow Quarry will reveal crinoidal limestone – a packed mass of fossil crinoids that when cut and polished produces the 'figure marble' that was so much in vogue during Victorian times.

Follow the dale down between limestone cliffs to Lathkill Head Cave, winter source of the River Lathkill. This huge cavity is generally dry in summer, with the River Lathkill trickling from a mine adit farther down, or in really dry weather from its bed even lower.

Continue to the junction with Cales Dale, where the route takes a footbridge to the right – though walkers who have arranged to be met by transport are encouraged to remain with the Lathkill and follow its beautiful course to Over Haddon or Alport.

However, on the main route follow the path up Cales Dale, climbing through a breach in the rockband via stiles to reach One Ash Grange. Originally a penitentiary for the monks of Roche Abbey, this attractive range of buildings includes a loft converted into a camping barn to provide cheap, acceptable accommodation.

Follow the farm-access track and pass Cales Farm to reach a cattle grid at the Long Rake road. Those who wish to visit the ancient monument of Arbor Low should turn right here and follow the road for ½ mile, then turn left up Upper Oldhams Farm track.

Returning to the entrance of Cales Farm, go diagonally left past the farm buildings and across pasture to a gate in the corner of the field. Continue along a track, dipping into an upper branch of Cales Dale, then continuing left beside a wall and through a gateway to another gate into a broad lane. This old way is known as Derby Lane, as confirmed by a stoop – or stone marker – that can be seen to the right of the track after the new gate.

Farther along the lane has a tarmac surface, then it meets Milking Lane by the Manor House at Rake End. Continue along the street and go through the churchyard. Turn left past The Hobbit (formerly The Black Bull) to return to the car park in Monyash.

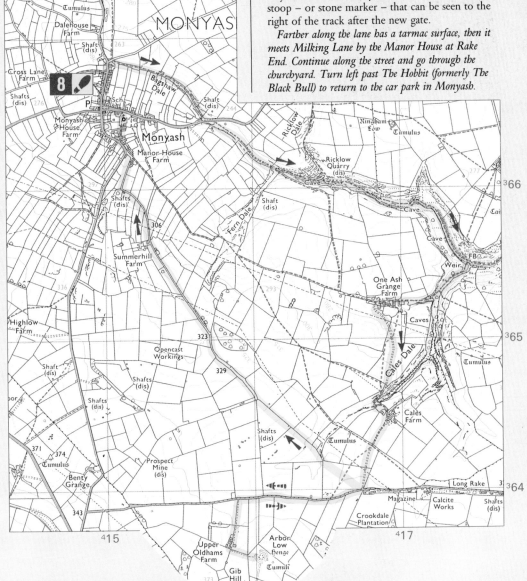

WALK 9
The Tissington and High Peak Trails

A kestrel – one of Britain's four species of falcon. These birds are a familiar sight in this part of the Peak

---

Allow at least 1½ hours

A gentler side of the White Peak is demonstrated by this walk, which uses the old railway track beds on which the popular Tissington and High Peak Trails are based to explore the green landscapes of the plateau 'table land'. The walking is good – and for that matter, so is the cycling.

From the Parsley Hay car park (SK147637) picnic site and bicycle-hire centre walk south for a short distance along the High Peak Trail, then fork right along another trackbed to join the Tissington Trail and enter the impressive Parsley Hay railway cutting. Continue to the second cutting. Here the fossil enthusiast may wish a pause to search the limestone face and fallen debris for brachiopods, crinoids and corals.

Continue along a fine embankment section, and after Hartington Moor Farm, enter a third cutting before crossing the Hand Dale viaduct and entering the former Hartington Station yard. The embankment section offers wide, open views across Long Dale to the hill of Carder Low. At the station yard is an old signal box that has been converted into an information centre. There are toilets too.

From the station yard go left along the approach road to join the B5054, and at that junction turn right to pass an abandoned lime kiln. Continue for a short way, cross the road and turn left on to a broad green lane heading away and uphill from the surfaced highway. Cross the busy A515 just 200yds short of The Jug and Glass pub and continue along the rough track to its intersection with the High Peak Trail. Stone, beehive-type kilns – often built into the hillside like the example passed on the way from Hartington Station yard – were used to burn limestone and make it sufficiently soluble to 'sweeten' acid pasture. The green lane is an excellent example of what must have once been an important road that changing fortunes has made redundant.

At the High Peak Trail turn left along the trackbed, pass through the thin band of Blakemoor Plantation and enter a cutting with a sharp bend – typical of this trail. Pass beneath the A515 through Newhaven Tunnel and return to the start. At each portal of the

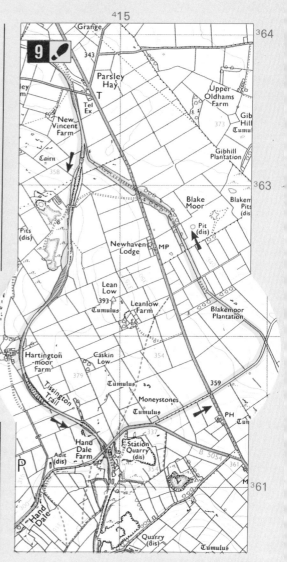

Newhaven Tunnel are original Cromford and High Peak Railway Company plaques, dated 1825. The northern of the two is the most elaborate, bearing the Latin motto *Divina Palladis Arte* and the names of principal engineer Josiah Jessop and company clerk William Brittlebank.

Part of the Tissington Trail, formerly a railway

Valley of the Upper Dove

Allow up to 3 hours

While south of charming Hartington village the banks of the River Dove are being trodden into mud by visitors flocking into Beresford Dale, the wider valley to the north is comparatively unfrequented, even though the walking is good.

Leaving the picturesque Market Square (SK128604) in Hartington, the walk heads north along Dig Street, which becomes a gated road that is followed all the way to a group of farm buildings on the right, known as the hamlet of Pilsbury. On the right at the third gate, before Pilsbury and short of Ludwell Farm, is a cave-like entrance. Not a cave and certainly not to be entered, this is an 'adit' tunnelled to drain lead mine shafts.

Just beyond Pilsbury farmstead a track leading on from where the real road hairpins back on itself leads past an open-sided barn on the left to the earthworks of Pilsbury Castle. The name Pilsbury strongly suggests that the Norman motte-and-bailey castle was built here on a Saxon site.

Return along the track to the road, and just beyond the Pilsbury farmhouse turn right and descend along a pasture edge to a footbridge over the Dove. Cross this and turn immediately right to climb a track for a short distance. Crossing the footbridge takes the walker from Derbyshire into Staffordshire, and from carboniferous limestone to the coarser gritstone that is evident in the craggy summit of Sheen Hill.

On the left of the track, just a little way up from the river and opposite a fixed gate, is a stile. Cross this and ascend diagonally to another stile that can be seen in the distance. Cross this, continue uphill to a wall and follow this along the side of the hill and cross another stile. Keep left to the first gateway, cross a stile near a barn in trees and cross another stile on to the Sheen road. Turn left along the road, and at a corner enter Harris Close farmyard, on the left. The footpath is marked by a sign on the righthand corner of the farm building farthest to the right. Between this and a stone wall is an unlikely-looking gap that is the path entrance. Continue along the downhill side of a curiously-banked wall, crossing two gates and two stiles before descending pasture to another stile.

After a while follow the edge path through the uphill fringes of a conifer plantation – watching out for slippery roots in wet weather – and on leaving the plantation slant gradually down the scarp bank through hawthorn scrub to the Sheen bridleway. Cross this track to a stile and gate. Cross the stile, the subsequent meadow and a footbridge over the Dove. Continue over more stiles to the car park of J M Nuttall's milk-processing factory and turn left along the access road to reach the Market Square in Hartington.

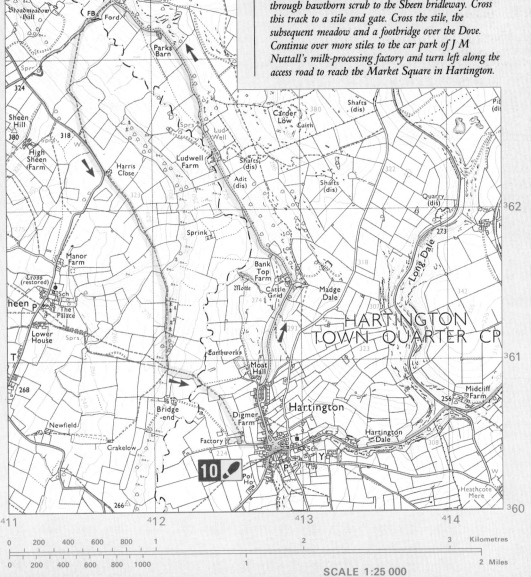

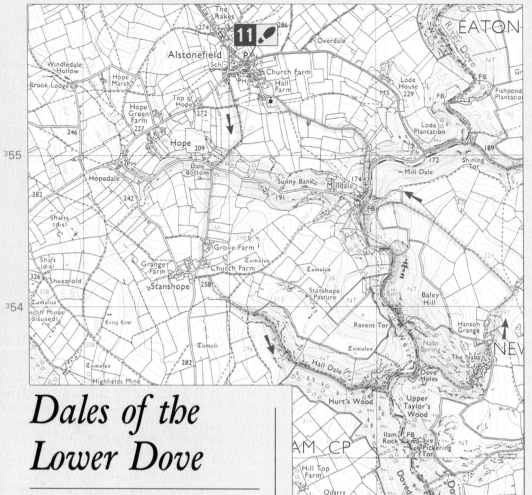

Dales of the Lower Dove

Allow at least 3½ hours

With a bit of effort – and be warned, for there certainly is effort involved – a far more balanced view of Dovedale and its attendant valleys can be enjoyed by approaching it from Alstonefield rather than via the usual routes from Thorpe or Ilam. That is what this often-strenuous walk does, dipping in and out of beautiful side dales while glimpsing Dovedale proper.

From the National Park car park in Alstonefield (SK131556) turn right, then after a very short distance right again into a road signposted 'Wetton'. Continue forward past picturesque houses and triangular greens to a T-junction opposite the old school, and turn left – then almost immediately left again past cottages into a green lane. Follow this to a severe right-hand bend, where the route continues straight on downhill beside a wall to the right. Bear right with the wall and descend very steeply to cross a minor road in Hopedale, then continue with a stiff climb up the other side along a green lane to the dairy-farm hamlet of Stanshope. On reaching the road in Stanshope turn left past the farm and immediately left again – also past the farm – on a rough track. A little way along find on the right a signpost indicating 'Dovedale'. Follow the path into Hall Dale via a series of easily-seen stiles, then follow Hall Dale itself to the River Dove. At the river turn right through a wall 'squeeze' stile and follow the bank to a footbridge in the shadows of Pickering Tor and Ilam Rock. At first green and softly pastoral, Hall Dale narrows into a deep, wild gorge with limestone terraces and buttresses towering either side of a steep path – often scattered with scree –

that plunges through woodland to join Dovedale. Here the main dale is guarded by the huge pinnacle of Pickering Tor and spire of Ilam Rock.

Cross the Dove footbridge and turn left along what is probably the most popular footpath in the White Peak, leading to Dove Holes. The last vestiges of an enormous cave system eroded by glacial melt waters, Dove Holes attract visitors in thousands.

A choice of route can be made here – along an even path through lovely riverside scenery directly to Milldale, or by a more arduous route to the same destination up the sickle-shaped and crag-bound Nabs Dale. This dry valley is entered by branching right at Dove Holes and making a stiff climb through rocky woodland to a stile at the edge of a field. Cross this and walk straight ahead a few yards to a double finger-post waymark. Facing the post turn left and cross a stile next to a farm gate opposite the farmhouse. Skirt the buildings of Hanson Grange Dairy Farm to join the farm-access track, and turn right to follow the track to a four-way fingerpost standing at the corner of a wall. From here leave the track by following the Milldale sign to the left and descend via stiles and alongside a wall to the viewpoint of Hanson Toot.

From Hanson Toot the path zig-zags down a steep incline to cross the bridge, then leaves the valley along Millway Lane – which is signposted on the shop as the way 'to the Chapel in the valley'. Actually, it goes all the way to Alstonefield Church, from where the green, The George Inn and car park are easily found. The lane has a sting in its tail – a long climb.

A Victorian Village

Allow up to 3 hours

Here at the threshold of the White Peak is a countryside where the height of artificiality is juxtaposed with a peaceful natural landscape – and the effect is marvellous. On one hand are the Victorian conceits of Ilam village and its hall, the former 'Alpine' and the latter 'Tudor Gothic'. On the other is the Manifold Valley, winding below high hilltops.

Leave the National Park Blore Pastures car park and picnic site (SK136497) by walking north and descending via stiles through pasture to an unenclosed but metalled road. Here turn right to continue downhill to a cattle grid. Cross this too, then walk over Ilam Bridge into Ilam. From the bridge go straight ahead into the village, meeting a drive to Ilam Hall. Follow this, then very shortly and before the gates fork left on to the Dove House drive. At the gates to Dove House turn left to follow a field-edge track to the church. When Jesse Watts-Russell rebuilt Ilam Hall in 1820 he completed his grand design by moving the whole village away from the church. Treasures here include two Saxon churchyard crosses and a pair of fine chapels. The hall itself is run jointly by the National Trust and Youth Hostels Association as an adventure centre, and includes a tea room.

The route can continue by descending steps to join the Paradise Walk near St Bertram's Bridge – or crossing the terraced gardens, passing the tea rooms and slanting down towards the river on a wooded path which skirts a stone grotto. Either way, the Paradise Walk is joined and followed upstream through the Manifold meadows and past the Battle Cross (read plaque) to a footbridge. The name of the river means literally many folds or meanders, but its old name of Ilam – meaning hill stream – is more descriptive. During dry weather it sinks into its bed upstream at Wettonmill, rising across the meadow from Paradise Walk at the Boil Hole (no public access). Its tributary The Hamps does the same trick, disappearing below ground at Waterfall (hence its name) and flowing through caves under Musden Low before emerging by Musden footbridge.

Either cross the footbridge and make the energetic climb direct from here to Musden Grange, or adopt the more sedate course of continuing along the river to River Lodge and paying the handsome price of one new penny to cross a private garden to the road. Once on the road continue alongside the river to Rushley Bridge. Cross this and ascend the track through Rushley Farm, bearing left to climb to Musden Grange. Keep right of the grange buildings, then where the track switches right slant left by an ascending wall. Go through a hedge gap above a small, tree-filled enclosure and ascend diagonally over pasture to a waymark at a fork. Keep left here and continue to climb diagonally and reach a gate with scrub on the left. Cross a stile here and work uphill alongside a wall to a stile into the yard of derelict Upper Musden farmstead. Note here the solid construction of the buildings, the tree-shelter belt and the circular mere – all vital elements for survival in such an exposed position. *Cross the stile left of the barn, then immediately cross another adjacent to it. Descend pasture along an old and sparse hedgeline to a gate and horse jump, then climb via gates along an obvious bridleway above Hinckley Wood. On reaching a minor road turn left and proceed for about 150yds to a gate and stile. Cross the stile and descend ridge-and-furrow pasture for the return to the car park.*

SCALE 1:25 000

WALK 13

Dippers, rarely far from water, can wade and swim

Sheep Walks Under the Water

Allow up to 2 hours

Before the creation of Fernilees and Errwood Reservoirs the great moorland pastures that swooped down dale sides to the River Goyt were sheep walks for no fewer than 15 farms. They were also the natural home of the tough Dale O'Goyt sheep, a distinctive speckled-faced breed known more popularly as the Derbyshire Gritstone. Today people come to wander the shores of peaceful reservoirs that cover lands where the flocks once grazed, and to stroll across the unflooded tops with only the calls of curlew and grouse for company.

Stop at the Derbyshire Bridge car park (SK017716) and climb gently east – or right for someone facing uphill – towards Burbage Edge and Buxton on a track known as the Macclesfield Old Road. Keen eyes will note several mounds of grey spoil along the way, evidence of mainly 19th-century pits that were worked for low-grade domestic coal.

Continue through the cleft of Berry Clough, pass an old milestone and climb to the crest of the ridge. Turn left here to follow a grass path through heather, accompanied by waymark posts bearing yellow arrows over which the number six has been superimposed. Open views of the upper Wye Valley around Buxton are enjoyed from the crest, and the ridgetop parade of posts interestingly coincides with the main watershed of England. Rain falling here drains east into streams that feed the Wye, thence the Derwent and Trent before reaching the North Sea via the Humber Estuary; and west to supply the Goyt for Liverpool's mighty Mersey and eventually the stormy Irish Sea.

Reach a point where the path divides and continue left, then reach a cairn and go left again to descend a re-entrant of Berry Clough. Keep to the north (left if facing downstream) bank of the clough, and after passing the foundations of a shooting cabin reach a footbridge spanning the youthful River Goyt. Cross the bridge, ascend to the valley road and follow this upstream to the starting point. In summer, when traffic densities in the valley are often very high, a one-way (uphill) system applies. Within 100yds a dry ditch merges with the road from the right – a leat that was created to feed an overshot waterwheel in Goyt's Clough Quarry. Its natural continuation towards the weir is visible, though breached. Prior to the establishment of a crushing mill the quarry was the original base for the Pickfords – a family firm that developed from mineral extraction and haulage into pre-eminence as a national removals company. Farther up the narrow clough – to the left beyond the cascades – can be seen an old mine level that was a private working belonging to the Grimshaw family of Errwood Hall.

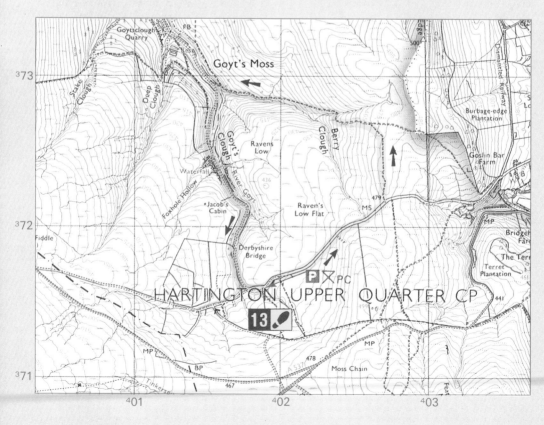

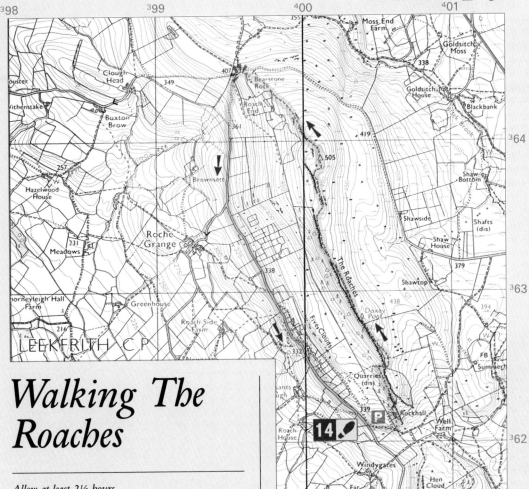

Walking The Roaches

Allow at least 2½ hours

Nothing to do with fish or insects, 'Roaches' is an unambiguous place name which comes from the French *le Roche* – simply indicating a rocky place. It is certainly that, but this region where Britain's high and lowlands meet in a wild tangle of soaring gritstone and boulder-strewn slopes has quiet paths that are easily found and enjoyed without undue exertion.

There is ample layby parking. (SK004621). Leave through a gate and follow a gravel track for a few hundred yards, ascending a small rise until the buildings of Rockhall Cottage come into view. This is the home of a recluse and is known locally as Doug's Abode. The next section follows a special 'bypass' around it. *Strike off on the path left of the gravel track, aiming for the left corner of the property. Pass close to the front door and through the first gap in the stone wall to enter a plantation. Climb to the base of the crags ahead, find steps to the left of the main crag and at the top of the first tier reach a wall.*

Turn left at the top of the steps, (without passing through the gap in the wall), and follow the path among huge boulders at the base of the overhanging cliffs. Continue to a Roaches Estate sign at a path junction, turn right, and walk uphill alongside a broken fence and wall into the gully breach. After a short scramble over loose rocks emerge on the ridge. Turn left along a clear path beside a stone wall which follows the ridge. After about ¼ mile pass the peaty shallows of Doxey Pool and gradually drop with the diminishing cliffs. Easily seen from here are Hen Cloud and the Ramshaw Rocks, both of which belong to the same intensely-folded strata of Millstone Grit as the rocks of the Roaches.

Farther along the path negotiates strangely-shaped, wind-streaked rocks showing typical cross bedding and climbs to 1,658ft summit marked by an OS trig pillar. Superb, panoramic views can be enjoyed from here. Dominating the northern hillscape are 1,659ft Shutlingsloe, rising over the ancient Goldsitch Moss coalfields; the Axe Edge moors soaring to 1,807ft east of The Three Shires Head; and Oliver's Head – at 1,684ft, the highest point in Staffordshire.

Descend through another band of sculpted stone to reach the most unbearlike Bearstone Rock, a notable viewpoint. It is worth pausing here to consider a scene that might be described as one of the country's best examples of the transition between lowland and the high country, from the soft greens of wood and pasture to the heather, cotton grass, bilberry and rocks that typify moorland.

Complete the descent to the Roach End Pass, at 1,322ft, and turn left down a minor road – initially through two gates. Along this road attention is focussed west through the Dane Gap to The Cloud, a hill rising to 1,126ft above Congleton. Beyond it undulates the Cheshire Plain.

Reach a road junction and turn left to ascend, with views of the fine old Roche Grange below to the right, soon rising below the Five Clouds sandstone buttress spurs and returning to the start. At its southern end the Five Clouds formation has been quarried for building stone – some of which was used to build the notable Rockhall Folly. The final stretch of the walk overlooks Tittesworth Reservoir, whose 19th-century dam was enlarged in 1963.

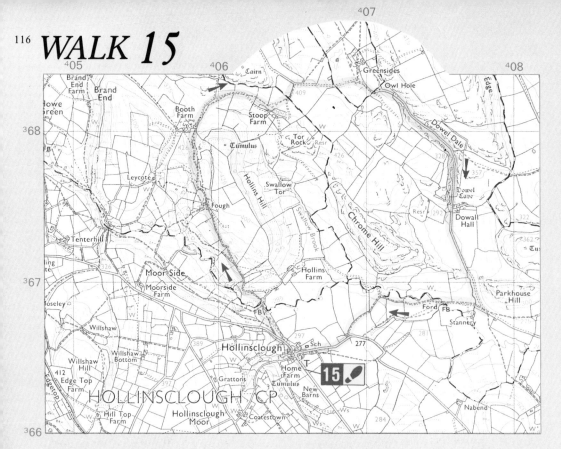

Near the Source of the Dove

Allow 2 hours

A Yorkshireman walking this route may well feel an overwhelming sense of deja-vu. For after climbing high over grassy hills from the infant Dove and dropping along a gated road the walk enters a natural amphitheatre irresistibly reminiscent of The Three Peaks. Here, however, the splendour is provided by soaring and isolated summits of reef limestone.

Parking is tricky, but space may be found along the road near the telephone box (SK066665) in Hollinsclough, a picturesque village beneath high hills. From the telephone box walk north-west past a chapel building on the right and wall post box on the left. After about 200yds and on an ascent reach a bridle gate on the right. Cross this and descend diagonally, at first beside a wall, to a packhorse bridge over the rushing infant Dove beside a Severn-Trent Water Authority flow gauge. Cross the river and the gate at the end of the bridge, then slant diagonally up rough pasture on the downhill side of a wall to meet a recognisable track. Follow this left and continue to climb. All along this rough road may be enjoyed superb views of the upper Dove Hills, dominated by Axe Edge and open in comparison with the verdant, tree-filled valley below.

Still climbing on the track, pass on the left a small collection of farm buildings known as Fough hamlet (pronounced Fuff), and continue to a cattle grid and sweeping right-hand curve that takes the route away from Booth Farm, down on the left. A booth was a sheltered corral in wild and exposed country.

Reach another cattle grid and branch right towards Stoop Farm, then just before the farm's tree-shelter belt climb diagonally left across pasture and above the farm buildings to reach another cattle grid and a track leading down to a gated road. A good landmark here is the bristly, craggy crest of Chrome Hill (no access), which rises conspicuously to the right.

Walk down the track to the unenclosed public road and turn right, passing through a gate and heading towards the access drive for Greenside Farm. The roadsides here, particularly opposite the farm track, are pitted with curious hollows known as swallets or swallow holes. These consume moorland rivers that plunge into their depths and enter an uncharted region of subterranean fissures to later rise again as the Dowel Stream.

Pass through a second gate, and staying with the road pass on the left near a corner a sad and tre-shrouded dump that used to be Owl Hole. Descend via gates through the lovely limestone-walled and riverless Dowel Dale to a gate by Dowel Hall. Just short of the gate and up on the right is the Dowel Cave, in which excavations have revealed evidence of Neolithic funerary practice. After the hall and a cattle grid the Dowel – or Dove Well – gushes from a source to the right of the path and flows alongside the road through a natural amphitheatre of mini mountain peaks. At the far end is a dramatic pass between 1,417ft Chrome Hill on the right and the 1,221ft bulk of Parkhouse Hill on the left. This secret place would be worth any amount of walking to find.

Continue through the amphitheatre, leaving by the pass, then after crossing a cattle grid and a conduit containing the Dowel Stream branch acutely back along a track that leaves the road from the right and drops through stone gateposts topped by spheres. Continue to a footbridge and ford on the River Dove, cross the bridge and continue alongside the river on a path that is grassy and indistinct at first, but which after a stile and gate becomes a metalled farm track. At the end of the track meet a minor road and turn right to pass the Frank Weldon Centre, thus completing the walk.

Manifold Woodlands

Allow at least 3½ hours

This is a long and in places energetic walk, with areas that can ben slippery and potentially tricky in wet weather. However, given those cautions it is one that will be remembered for the great gap of Thor's Cave, yawning out over the thickly-wooded Manifold Valley.

From the National Park car park (SK109552) in Wetton head a short way south to the nearby road junction, turn right, then meet a second junction and turn left along a green lane signposted 'concessionary path to Thor's Cave'. Follow this to a stile and gate, cross the stile, then follow a sign right to another stile. Keep close to the upper wall, descending briefly (and in the wet messily) before ascending to a fence stile, from which an often slippery path runs to the cave.

At this point some walkers ascend to the precipitous crag above Thor's Cave for the admittedly splendid views over the Manifold Valley and farther. In wet weather such an exercise could prove highly dangerous. Likewise, care should be taken on the path to the cave itself, and the ensuing descent into the valley bottom.

Used since prehistory for various purposes, the cave has a tilted bedrock floor and can be entered without too much difficulty. The great fissure known as the West Window leads to nothingness and must not be descended.

Descend from the cave, initially with promising-looking steps but subsequently down a steep and potentially messy scramble to the valley floor. At the bottom go straight ahead to the footbridge over the Manifold – or in summer, the bed where it used to be.

From the footbridge cross the Manifold Track and climb the slope opposite through Ladyside Wood, with views of the Thor's Cave outcrop featuring large behind. The Manifold Track was a breakthrough in recreational facilities when in the 1930s Staffordshire County Council surfaced the trackbed of the light railway that ran there until 1934. *Reach a field edge, cross to the wood edge on the left and re-enter the wood by a ladder stile. Continue for a fair distance along a level though rocky path to another stile by a stone trough. Cross this, slant left up pasture to a hedge stile and cross a tiny rivulet before crossing a gate and stile into a short lane. Turn right here and continue to Grindon green and church.*

Cross the green in front of the church and meet a road opposite a skimpy modern mere and new picnic site. Turn right down the road, then before Ossom's Hill Farm branch left over a stile by a gate and descend through fields into the Hoo Valley via stiles and gates. Cross a footbridge and follow the stream down the valley (beware of bulls) by means of further stiles and gates to Wettonmill Camping Site. Meet the road by a ford, go left and cross Wettonmill Bridge, then turn right to enter Wettonmill yard – where there is a café. A gate beyond and behind the millhouse gives access to a ridge that must be crossed from side to side (not lengthways) to reach a bridle gate half obscured by vegetation. Follow the path from this gate into a broad, dry valley and ascend gently to a gate and stile by Ecton Manor House. The valley is splendidly peaceful. Hares are seen here, bounding up scree-scattered slopes amongst the pale blue of harebells.

Opposite Ecton Manor House go right, cross the stream and then ascend alongside a wall before following a line of stiles over the shoulder of Wetton Hill and on to a lane leading into Wetton village.

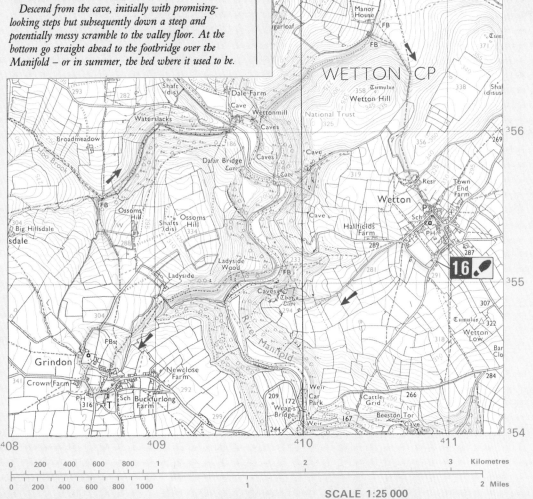

Index

Page numbers in bold type indicate main entries. Those in brackets indicate tours and walks.

Acknowledgements

The publishers would like to thank the many individuals who helped
in the preparation of this book. Special thanks are due to the
Peak National Park Authority.

The Automobile Association wishes to thank the following photographers,
organisations and libraries. Many of the photographs reproduced are the copyright of
the AA Picture Library.

M Aldelman 39 Pavilion Gardens, 39 Opera House, 100 Arkwright Mill Cromford, 100 Riber Castle Snowy Owl;
Arkwrights 43 R Arkwright; *M Birkett* 1 Stone Walling, 5 High Tor Matlock, 7 Arbor Low, 9 Narrow Fields Chelmorton,
9 Monsal Viaduct, 9 Goyt Bridge, 10 Peak National Park Sign, 13 Chelmorton, 14 Tissington Trail, 22 Peak Cavern,
23 Well Dressing Hope, 24 Morris Dancer Headgear, 25 Love Feast, 31 Heights of Abraham Cable Cars,
33 Maids' Garland in Church, 34 View from Axe Edge, 34 Lead Font in Church, 35 View across Bridge Bakewell,
35 Bakewell Pudding Sign, 36 View from Baslow Edge, 36 Victoria 1897 Clock, 36/37 View from Beeley Moor,
37 Market Place Bonsall, 38 Spring Water Label, 40 Stalactites Treak Cliff Caves, 40 Winnat's Pass, 40/41 Stocks –
Chapel-en-le-Frith, 41 Narrowfields Chelmorton, 42 Crooked Spire Chesterfield, 44/45 Children crossing river, 45 Old Nag's Head,
46 Riley Graves Eyam, 47 Village Pond Foolow, 47 Old Glossop, 48 Haddon Hall, 48 Goyt Valley, 48 Bridge Grindleford,
49 Howden Dam, 50 Kinder Downfall, 51 'Nora Batty's' Holmfirth, 51 Compo Wellies Money Box,
52 Thor's Cave, 53 1723 House Litton, 53 Dried up bed River Manifold, 54 Longnor Market Place,
54 Longshaw Moorland Estate, 55 Lyme Park, 55 Orangery Lyme Park, 55 Fishing Ridgegate Reservoir,
56 View from Heights of Abraham, 56 Cable Cars, 57 Miller's Dale, 57 Eldon Hole, 58 Fere Mere, 59 Conkesbury Bridge,
60 Peak Forest, 60 Mill Rowsley, 61 Peacock Hotel Rowsley, 61 Rudyard Lake, 62 Stanton Moor, 63 Stoney Middleton,
63 Curber, 64 Taddington Dale, 64 Tideswell Church, 65 Longendale, 66 Tissington Trail, 66 Farming, 67 Fenny Bentley,
67 Gradbach, 68 Winster, 69 Bradford Dale, 69 Youlgreave Church, 70 Errwood Reservoir, 71 Chapel-en-le-Frith,
73 Magpie Mine, 74 Peak District Mining Museum, 75 Start of Pennine Way, 75 Walkers Ashopton Valley,
76 Steam Traction Engine, 77 Winnats Pass, 96 Peveril Castle, 96 Peak Cavern, 97 Mam Tor, 98 Chatsworth House Cascades,
98 Making Bakewell Tarts, 99 Chatsworth House Outside; *C Daniel* 20 Women Mineworker, 25 Ilam Church Funeral Garland; *Mansell Collection* Back Cover Peak Cavern,
106 Mountain Hare; *Mary Evans Picture Library* 39 Buxton Crescent, 114 Dipper; *Nature Photographs* 16 Ling & Bell Heather
(FVB), 16 Emperor Moth (P Sterry), 16 Bog Asphodel (P Sterry), 18 Wheatear (P Sterry); *R Newton* 8 Eyam Cross,
32 Arbor Low, 33 Blue John Stone, 35 Bakewell Tarts, 41 Chatsworth House – Gardens, 52 Thor's Cave Manifold Valley,
70 Blue John, 72 Speedwell Cavern, 73 Eagle Owl; *H Parker* 19 Gollonda Mine 1907, 20 Mr Fox Entombed,
20 Standard Dish, 21 Mandale Sough, 21 Millclose Mine; *Peak National Park* Front Cover Monsal Dale, 6 Stannage,
7 Dew Pond, 10/11 Snake Pass Towards Kinder, 11 Notice, 11 Mass Trespass, 12 Upper Derwent, 15 Dove Valley,
16/17 Cotton Grass, 19 Magpie Mine, 24 Litton Well Dressing, 25 Castleton Garlanding, 26 Rush Bearing,
27 Walking in the Dark Peak, 27 Ian Hurst on Patrol, 28 Meeting School Party, 28 Briefing of Rangers, 29 Ian Hurst,
30 Erecting Footpath Signs, 57 Peak Cavern, 99 Chatsworth House Outside; *J Russell* 17 Meadow Cranesbill,
18 Bloody Cranesbill, 44 Kingfisher; *Trevor Wood* 3 Crich Trams, 39 Crescent – Buxton, 42 Crich Tramway Museum,
43 Arkwright's Mill, 74 Crich Tramway Museum; *Tim Woodcock* 50 Little John's Grave Hathersage

Other Ordnance Survey Maps of the Peak District

How to get there with Routemaster and Routeplanner Maps

Reach the Peak District from Lancaster, Newcastle, York, Peterborough, Birmingham and
Liverpool using Routemaster map sheets 5 and 6. Alternatively use the Ordnance Survey Great
Britain Routeplanner Map which covers the whole country on one map sheet.

Exploring with Landranger, Tourist and Outdoor Leisure Maps

Landranger Series
1¼ inches to one mile or 1:50,000 scale

These maps cover the whole of Britain and are good
for local motoring and walking. Each contains
tourist information such as parking, picnic places,
viewpoints and rights of way. Sheets covering the
Peak District are:

109 Manchester
110 Sheffield and Huddersfield
118 Stoke-on-Trent and Macclesfield
119 Buxton, Matlock and Dovedale

Tourist Map Series
1 inch to one mile or 1:63,360 scale

These maps cover popular holiday areas and are
ideal for discovering the countryside. In addition to
normal map detail ancient monuments, camping and
caravan sites, parking facilities and viewpoints are
marked. Lists of selected places of interest are
included on some sheets and others include useful
guides to the area.

Tourist Map Sheet 4 covers the Peak District

Outdoor Leisure Map Series
2½ inches to one mile or 1:25,000 scale

These maps cover popular leisure and recreation
areas of the country and include details of Youth
Hostels, camping and caravanning sites, picnic areas,
footpaths and viewpoints.

Outdoor Leisure Map Sheets 1 and 24 cover the
Peak District

Other titles available in this series are:

Channel Islands	Ireland	North York Moors
Cornwall	Lake District	Scottish Highlands
Cotswolds	New Forest	Yorkshire Dales
	Northumbria	